contents

[introduction]

There has been such good response to *Domino Knitting* (Interweave, 2002) that I felt compelled to expand on those techniques and give readers even more ideas for this relaxing, but exciting, type of knitting. You don't need to be an expert knitter to knit domino squares—all you need to know is how to cast on, knit, purl, decrease, and bind off. Best of all, each square involves relatively few stitches and only minimal attention before the unique shapes take hold. But be prepared—this is an addictive form of knitting! One square leads to another, which leads to another, and so on.

I always keep a basket of colorful yarn and a pair of needles close at hand. Whenever the inspiration strikes, I pick up a couple of colors and knit a square. Before I know it, a design comes to life. Some of my designs are based on serendipity and others result from careful planning and development. Either way, I build square upon square to form blocks that become the foundations for all sorts of fascinating projects.

I generally like to knit my squares at a looser gauge than might be suggested by the yarn manufacturer so that I can felt the finished project in the washing machine. Not only does machine felting tighten up the stitches to make a dense fabric, it also hides small mistakes or uneven stitches!

SQUARES

Knitted squares form the foundation for domino projects. A square begins with an odd number of stitches and is shaped by working double decreases on the center three stitches of every other row. The size of a square depends on the number of stitches in the first row—the more stitches, the larger the square. Most of the squares in this book are worked in garter stitch (every row is knitted), which produces a subtle texture pattern that is particularly well suited for stripes.

BLOCKS

All of the projects in this book begin with blocks, which are composed of squares worked one on top of another to form panels. Panels are worked side by side (always from left to right) to form a block. In general, a block has the same number of squares across the base as along the height. For example, a block may consist of 4 squares (2 squares wide by 2 squares tall), 9 squares (3 squares wide by 3 squares tall), 16 squares (4 squares wide by 4 squares tall), etc. A small block may even consist of a single square.

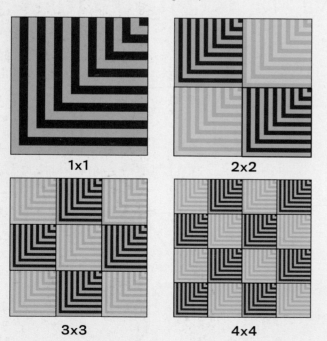

1x1   2x2

3x3   4x4

SPECIAL TECHNIQUES & ABBREVIATIONS

A number of special techniques and abbreviations are used in domino knitting. These are highlighted the first time they occur in each project and are fully explained in the Glossary on pages 134–140.

GAUGE AND MEASURING

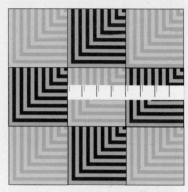

The gauge specified for each project is based on the dimensions of a single square. Because squares are always attached to other squares, you'll get the most accurate results if you measure your gauge on the center square of a panel of three squares (or better yet, in the center of a block of nine squares). When measuring widths, always measure horizontally between the centers of two squares oriented so that the first row of stitches is along the bottom and the last row is at the top.

FREQUENTLY ASKED QUESTIONS

There are a number of questions that come up every time I teach a domino workshop. Review these questions before you begin to ensure success every step along the way.

◤ What are domino needles?

Domino needles are straight needles that are only about 8" (20 cm) long. They have a knob on one end so that stitches can't fall off and so that the needles won't get stuck in the knitting or your clothing. You can substitute double-pointed needles but be careful not to let the stitches fall off the end. Because they are short, domino needles require less arm movement when turning the work as you knit the squares, and therefore you can knit longer without strain.

How many stitches does a square begin with?

You begin a square with any odd number of stitches. An odd number is needed so that there will be a center stitch, about which double decreases are worked.

Are squares always worked in garter stitch?

No, not necessarily. But because the simple relationship between the number of stitches and rows per inch in garter stitch, it's ideal for knitting true squares. You can use other stitch patterns, but the finished piece may not measure the same dimension in width and height (i.e., it may be rectangular instead of square).

How many stitches do I pick up and knit along a square when joining?

To maintain the correct dimensions of a square, you should pick up and knit the same number of stitches that are on each side of the center stitch of the first row. For example, if a square began with 25 stitches, you'll want to pick up and knit 12 stitches along each side, and 1 stitch in the center stitch for a total of 25 stitches picked-up (in garter stitch, this translates to 1 stitch for every garter ridge). But many squares begin with the last stitch of the previous square, which counts as the first picked-up stitch.

Why do you always specify the knitted cast-on?

The knitted cast-on tends to be looser than some other methods, and in domino knitting it's important that the cast-on stitches have the same tension as the knitted stitches. Also, the knitted method can be used to begin a row of knitting or to add stitches on either side of stitches that are already on the needle.

What's the importance of edge stitches?

The first stitch of every row (except the first row after casting on) is slipped, and the last stitch is always purled to make tidy edge stitches that are easy to identify when picking up and knitting stitches along the edges of the squares when forming a panel or block. The edge stitches are also nice when used for two-row stripes—there is one edge stitch for each two-row stripe— especially when worked as a twisted selvedge (see Glossary, page 137).

Can I use any yarn?

Because most of the projects in this book are felted after they're knitted, you'll want to use a wool yarn that will felt. Acrylic, polyester, cotton, and super-wash wool will not felt. If you're unsure whether or not a yarn will felt, knit up a sample square and run it through the washing machine just like you would the finished project. If the piece comes out of the washing machine smaller and denser, it has felted. To test the amount of felting, measure the square before and after running it through the machine.

Should I be concerned if I can't duplicate the finished measurements specified for the projects?

Because the degree of felting depends on several factors—water temperature, water chemistry, and amount of agitation—it's not unusual for different washing machines to produce different results. For this reason, the measurements for the projects in this book are provided as guidelines. None of the projects depend on precise measurements so don't be concerned if yours turn out a bit different than mine. I've included measurements before and after felting at the beginning of each project so you'll know what to aim for.

Can I use yarns leftover from other projects?

Absolutely! These projects can be made with a variety of yarn sizes and textures. Feel free to make substitutions—just be sure to knit a test square so you'll know how many stitches to cast on to get squares the same size as mine (or accept that your piece may be considerably different in size).

How do I change the size of a block?

One way to adjust the size is to change the number of stitches in the individual squares. For example, you can make each square larger by beginning with more stitches, or you can make each smaller by beginning with fewer stitches. You can also change the size of a block by working more or fewer squares in the block. For example, if the squares are the same size, a block made up of 16 squares will be larger than a block made up of 9 squares.

chapter one
knit squares and blocks

All of the projects in this book begin with an individual knitted square. The square can begin with any odd number of stitches—the more stitches, the larger the square. Additional squares are then worked on top of and adjacent to the first square to form larger blocks that become the foundations for a variety of projects, such as scarves, stoles, hot pads, and pillows.

THE CENTER TIP

After working just a few rows of a square, a point will form at the center (where you worked the decreases) of the lower edge. This point marks the center stitch of the square and can help alert you to when to work decreases on subsequent rows. Simply knit to the stitch before the center stitch, then work the double decrease on the next three stitches (slip 1 stitch knitwise, knit 2 stitches together, pass the slipped stitch over the knitted stitches and off the needle), then knit to the end of the row.

SQUARE SIZE

The number of stitches specified for the squares in a project will determine how the stitches are cast on and/or picked up and knitted. The same number of stitches fall on each side of the center stitch and the double decreases used to shape the squares are centered over the center stitch. A few examples are listed here.

21 stitches:
10 side stitches + 1 center stitch + 10 side stitches

23 stitches:
11 side stitches + 1 center stitch + 11 side stitches

25 stitches:
12 side stitches + 1 center stitch + 12 side stitches

27 stitches:
13 side stitches + 1 center stitch + 13 side stitches

29 stitches:
14 side stitches + 1 center stitch + 14 side stitches

31 stitches:
15 side stitches + 1 center stitch + 15 side stitches

33 stitches:
16 side stitches + 1 center stitch + 16 side stitches

35 stitches:
17 side stitches + 1 center stitch + 17 side stitches

37 stitches:
18 side stitches + 1 center stitch + 18 side stitches

39 stitches:
19 side stitches + 1 center stitch + 19 side stitches

41 stitches:
20 side stitches + 1 center stitch + 20 side stitches

43 stitches:
21 side stitches + 1 center stitch + 21 side stitches

HOW TO KNIT A SQUARE

Use the knitted method (abbreviated **K-CO**) to cast on the specified number of stitches. (The square shown here began with 25 stitches.)

Row 1: (WS) Knit to the last st, p1 *(edge st)*. **Note:** The first stitch (edge st) of subsequent rows will always be slipped, but you need to anchor it by knitting it on Row 1.

Row 2: (RS) Sl 1 kwise (edge st), knit to 1 st before the center st (in this case, k10), *sl 1 kwise, k2tog (the center st plus the next st), psso,* knit to the last st (in this case, k10), p1 (edge st)—2 sts decreased.

Row 3: Sl 1 kwise, knit to the last st, p1.

Row 4: Sl 1 kwise, knit to 1 st before the center st, sl 1 kwise, k2tog, psso, knit to the last st, p1—2 sts decreased.

Repeat Rows 3 and 4, working 1 st fewer before and after center st on RS rows, until 3 sts rem, ending with Row 4.

Next row: (WS) Sl 1 kwise, k1, p1.

Next row: (RS) Sl 1 kwise, k2tog, psso—1 st rem *(end st)*. This end st will become the first st of the next square (it doesn't matter if the next square will be a different color).

READING CHARTS

Each project has a chart that maps out the individual squares and how they relate to each other. The squares are numbered according to the order in which they are worked, beginning with Square 1. The orientation of the numbers indicates the direction of knitting (i.e., the numbers are shown right side up according to the knitting direction). In general, the squares are worked one on top of another to form panels and the panels are worked side by side, with the new panels worked on the right edge of existing panels. (However, this doesn't apply to squares that are added in rounds as for the Dotted Tea Cozy on page 70.) For projects that involve more than one color, the colors are specified with letters along with the number of the squares. For example, 3/E indicates that the third square is worked with color or color sequence E. The colors are identified with each chart.

Many of the projects in this book involve squares and blocks joined to each other to form three-dimensional shapes. Before you begin a project, make a photocopy of the chart, then fold and tape it together into the three-dimensional shape of the finished project. This will help you see how the squares relate to each other as they are knitted.

HOW TO JOIN SQUARES INTO A BLOCK

Squares are worked in panels to form blocks according to the sequence provided in the chart. For a 16-square block, the squares are worked in a series of 4 panels, each consisting of 4 squares. For the first panel, the squares are worked one on top of the other. Similarly, the squares in the second panel are worked one on top of another, but they are also attached to the right edge of the first panel as they are knitted. Likewise, the third panel is worked along the right edge of the second panel and the fourth panel is worked along the right edge of the third.

To practice knitting and joining squares to form a 16-square block, gather three colors of sportweight yarn and needles suitable for this yarn weight (sizes U.S. 3 to 5 [3.25 to 3.75 mm]). In the sample shown, MC is light lavender, CC1 is navy, and CC2 is rose. Each square is worked in two colors, with the colors changing every two rows (the cast-on row counts as one row). **Note:** *See the glossary (pages 133–140) for abbreviations and highlighted terms.*

PANEL 1
‹ *Square 1*
With MC, **K-CO** 25 sts.
Row 1: (WS) Knit to the last st, p1 *(edge st)*.
Row 2: (RS) Change to CC1. Sl 1 kwise (edge st), k10, **sl 1 kwise, k2tog, psso,** k10, p1 (edge st)—23 sts.
Row 3: Sl 1 kwise, knit to the last st, p1.

Row 4: Change to MC. Sl 1 kwise, knit to 1 st before the center st (i.e., k9), sl 1 kwise, k2tog, psso, knit to the last st (i.e., k9), p1—21 sts.
Row 5: Sl 1 kwise, knit to the last st, p1.
Rep Rows 4 and 5, changing colors every RS row and working 1 st fewer before and after the center st, until 3 sts rem on a RS row.
Next row: (WS) Sl 1 kwise, k1, p1.
Next row: Do not change colors. Sl 1 kwise, k2tog, psso—1 st rem (end st). This becomes the first st of the next square.

‹ *Square 2*
Rotate Square 1 so that the left selvedge edge is at the top and so that the end st is at the upper right corner. With CC2 and 1 st already on the needle (the end st from Square 1), pick up and knit (abbreviated **pick-knit**) 11 sts sts across the upper edge of Square 1, beginning with the second st from the right edge and picking up under both loops of the MC edge-sts along the way (pick-knit 1 st for each garter ridge), then go **"around the corner"** and pick-knit 1 st in the nearest CO loop, turn the work around (abbreviated **turn work**), and K-CO 12 new sts—25 sts total. Work as for Square 1, working the first row with CC2, then alternating 2 rows each of MC and CC2.

‹ *Square 3*
Using the end st of Square 2 as the first st of Square 3, with MC, pick-knit 11 sts across the upper edge of Square 2, 1 st "around the corner," turn work, and K-CO 12 new sts—25 sts total. Work as Square 2, repeating the color sequence used for Square 1.

‹ *Square 4*
Using the end st of Square 3 as the first st of Square 4, with CC2, pick-knit 11 sts across the upper edge of Square 3, 1 st "around the corner," turn work, and K-CO 12 new sts—25 sts total. Work as for Square 2, but pull the end st loose, cut the yarn, and pull the tail through it.

WEAVE IN TAILS AS YOU KNIT

You can weave in the yarn tails as you knit by working them along a right-side row. Use this method to weave in as many tails as possible to reduce the number you'll have to weave in with a tapestry needle later. To prevent bulky tangles when you weave in a series of tails, always weave in the lowest-most tail first. Knit a few rows after weaving in tails, then trim the tails so about 3/8" (1 cm) hangs on the wrong side (this will prevent the tails from eventually slipping to the right side). The woven-in tails will lie along the wrong side and will not be visible on the right side of the work. Whether you hold the yarn in your left hand for the Continental method of knitting or in your right hand for the English method of knitting, hold the work as you would for Fair Isle knitting.

[figure 1]

[figure 2]

Continental Method

Hold the tail of the old color (white in the drawings) over your index finger and hold the new color (gray in the drawings) over both your index and middle finger, to the right of the old color (i.e., closer to your finger tips). * Insert the needle under the old yarn (figure 1) and knit one stitch with the new yarn, bring the needle over the old yarn (figure 2) and knit the next stitch with the new yarn; repeat from * two or three times.

English Method

Hold the tail of the old color on your left index finger and the new color with on your right index finger. *Insert the needle under the old color, throw the new color around the needle, bring the needle under the old color and knit the next stitch with the new color, then knit the next stitch as usual; repeat from * two or three times.

PANEL 2
Work a series of squares along the right edge of Panel 1 as follows.

‹ *Square 5*
With CC2, K-CO 12 sts, place the needle in your right hand (i.e., turn work), go "around the corner" *under* Square 1 and pick-knit 1 st in the far right CO loop of Square 1 (the lower-most square in Panel 1), then pick-knit 12 more sts evenly spaced (1 st after each garter ridge) along the right edge of Square 1, picking up through both loops of the edge sts except in the last st, in which you may only be able to catch the upper loop. Work as for Square 1 but slip the first st of Row 1 pwise with the yarn in front (wyf)
‹ *Square 6*
Using the end st of Square 5 as the first st of Square 6, with MC, pick-knit 11 sts along the upper edge of Square 5 (12 sts on right needle), 1 st in the upper right tip of Square 1, then 12 sts along the right edge of Square 2—25 sts total. Work for Square 1 but slip the first st of Row 1 pwise wyf.

‹ Square 7

Using the end st from Square 6 as the first st of Square 7, with CC2, pick-knit 11 sts along the upper edge of Square 6 (12 sts on right needle), 1 st in the upper right tip of Square 2, then 12 sts along the right edge of Square 3—25 sts total. Work as for Square 6, alternating 2 rows each of CC2 and MC.

‹ Square 8

Using the end st from Square 7 as the first st of Square 8, with MC, pick-knit 11 sts along the upper edge of Square 7 (12 sts on right needle), 1 st in the upper right tip of Square 3, then 11 sts along the right edge of Square 4, and 1 st in the end st of Square 4 (pull the end-st tail tight to secure this st). Work as for Square 6, alternating 2 rows each of MC and CC1, and end by pulling the end st loose, cutting the yarn, and threading the tail through it.

PANEL 3

Work as for Square 5, Square 6, Square 7, and Square 8 of Panel 2, CO 12 new sts for Square 9, then picking up sts along the edges of Square 5, Square 6, Square 7, and Square 8, respectively, and following the color sequence used for Panel 1.

PANEL 4

Work as for Square 5, Square 6, Square 7, and Square 8 of Panel 2, CO 12 new sts for Square 13, then picking up sts along the edges of Square 9, Square 10, Square 11, and Square 12, respectively, and following the color sequence used for Panel 2. **BO** the end st of Square 16.

MAKE A CHAIR CUSHION

To make a warm and comfortable cushion for your chair, follow the instructions above for a single block but use bulky wool yarn. The pad shown here was made from Rowan Big Wool (100% wool; 87 yd [80 m]/100 g) in #03 Smitten Kitten (light lavender; 2 balls), #26 Blue Velvet (navy; 1 ball), #14 Whoosh (rose; 1 ball) on U.S. size 15 (10 mm) needles. Before felting, each square measured about 5½" by 5½" (14 by 14 cm); after felting, each square measured about 3¼" by 3¼" (8.5 by 8.5 cm). The completed block was edged with strips of woven cotton fabric, which was also used to make two ties to secure the pad to the back of the chair.

PHOTO *Vivian Høxbro*

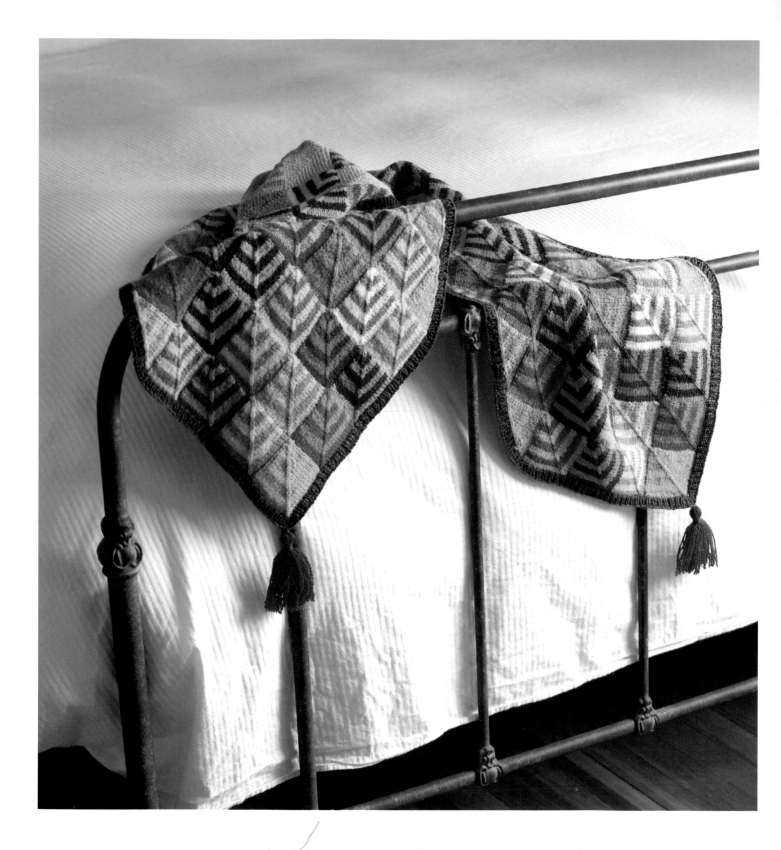

candy stole

This brightly colored shawl in a rainbow of candy colors reminds me of the happy hippie days of the 1960s. It is based on squares built one upon another in a series of diagonal panels that begin and/or end with triangles to make the long edges straight. The stole is worked in two pieces that are joined at the center. You can think of the overall arrangement as two and a half sixteen-square blocks with repeating color patterns and four half blocks with repeating color patterns in each of the two pieces. A ribbed edging is worked around the entire stole, but you could substitute a crocheted edge or a sewn-on edging of colorful bias binding. A bright tassel finished off each pointed end.

[materials]

FINISHED SIZE About 16" (41 cm) wide and 75¼" (191 cm) long, with edging, after blocking.

YARN Fingering weight (#1 Super Fine) in 19 colors.

Shown here: Harrisville New England Knitter's Shetland (100% wool; 217 yd [200 m]/50 g): Lady Slipper, Marigold, Seagreen, Cornsilk, Pink, Gold, Lime, Melon, Periwinkle, Poppy, Mustard, Foliage, Lilac, Grass, Cornflower, Magenta, Iris, White, and Bermuda Blue, 1 skein each. *Note:* This is enough yarn to make two stoles.

NEEDLES Size 3 mm (between U.S. size 2 and 3): domino needles (page 6) plus about 6 circular needles for working the edging. Exact gauge isn't important.

NOTIONS Removable stitch marker; tapestry needle; cardboard form for making tassels.

GAUGE

Each square measures 2½" by 2½" (6.5 by 6.5 cm) before blocking; 2¾" by 2¾" (7 by 7 cm) after blocking. Along the diagonal, each square measures 3½" (9 cm) wide and 3¼" (8.5 cm) high before blocking; 4" (10 cm) wide and 3¾" (9.5 cm) high after blocking.

[techniques]

- ◤ knit squares and blocks (page 9)
- ◤ reading charts (page 10)
- ◤ join squares into a block (page 11)
- ◤ weave in tails as you knit (page 12)
- ◤ See Glossary (page 133) for abbreviations and highlighted terms.

[notes]

▶ Work the squares and triangles in numerical order and in the colors specified on the chart.

▶ Work the two-color squares in stockinette stitch; work the solid-color squares in garter stitch. For the two-color squares, change colors every fourth row (the cast-on and/or pick-up row counts as one row).

▶ The direction of the numbers on the chart indicates the knitting direction

▶ The chart represents one-half of the stole; work the colors as listed in the color sequence.

▶ Before blocking, the piece will be wavy and the squares will lie on top of one another like the leaves of an artichoke.

▶ To maintain straight edges, triangles are worked between the squares along each edge of the scarf.

FIRST HALF
PANEL 1
‹ *Square 1*

With Lady Slipper, **K-CO** 31 sts. Work in stockinette stitch in striped sequence (alternating colors every 4 rows) as foll:

Row 1: (WS) Purl.

Row 2: (RS) Sl 1 kwise (**edge st**), knit to 1 st before center st (i.e., k13), sl 2 sts tog kwise, k1, pass the 2 slipped sts over the knit st (p2sso), knit to last st (i.e., k13), p1 (edge st)—29 sts.

Row 3 and all foll WS rows: Sl 1 kwise, purl to end.

Row 4: Change to Marigold. Sl 1 kwise, k12, sl 2 sts tog kwise, k1, p2sso, k12, p1—27 sts.

Row 6: Sl 1 kwise, k11, sl 2 sts tog kwise, k1, p2sso, k11, p1—25 sts.

Row 8: Change to Lady Slipper. Sl 1 kwise, k10, sl 2 sts tog kwise, k1, p2sso, k10, p1—23 sts.

Row 10: Sl 1 kwise, k9, sl 2 sts tog kwise, k1, p2sso, k9, p1—21 sts.

COLOR SEQUENCE FOR FIRST HALF

Square 1: Lady Slipper and Marigold.

Square 2: Seagreen and Cornsilk.

Square 3: Pink and Gold.

Square 4: Lime and Periwinkle.

Triangle 5: Marigold and Lady Slipper.

Square 6: Poppy and Mustard.

Square 7: Lilac and Grass.

Square 8: Cornflower and Marigold.

Square 9: Magenta and Gold.

Square 10: Mustard and Poppy.

Triangle 11: Grass and Lilac.

Square 12: Cornflower and Magenta.

Square 13: Pink and Foliage.

Square 14: Lime and Melon.

Square 15: Lilac and Iris.

Square 16: Magenta and Cornflower.

Square 17: Foliage and Pink.

Triangle 18: Melon and Lime.

Square 19: Cornsilk and Grass

Square 20: White and Bermuda Blue.

Square 21: Periwinkle and Seagreen.

Square 22: Poppy and Lady Slipper.

Square 23: Grass and Cornsilk.

Square 24: Bermuda Blue and White.

Square 25: Seagreen and Periwinkle.

Triangle 26: Lady Slipper and Poppy.

Triangle 27: Marigold and Lady Slipper.

Square 28: Cornsilk and Seagreen.

Square 29: Gold and Pink.

Square 30: Periwinkle and Lime.

Squares and Triangle 31 to 35: As for Squares and Triangle 1 to 5.

Triangle 36: Grass and Lilac.

Square 37: Marigold and Cornflower.

Square 38: Gold and Magenta.

Squares 39 to 44: As for Squares 6 to 11.

Triangle 45: Melon and Lime.

Square 46: Iris and Lilac.

Squares and Triangle 47 to 53: As for Squares and Triangle 12 to 18.

Triangle 54: Lady Slipper and Poppy.

Squares 55 to 60: As for Squares 19 to 24.

Square 61: Grass.

Squares and Triangle 62 to 68: As for Squares and Triangle 27 to 33.

Squares and Triangle 69 to 71: As for Squares and Triangle 36 to 38.

Square 72: Cornflower.

Square 73: Lilac and Grass.

Square 74: Seagreen.

Squares and Triangle 75 to 77: As for Squares and Triangle 45 to 47.

Triangle 78: Lady Slipper and Poppy.

Square 79: Lime.

Triangle 80: Marigold and Lady Slipper.

COLOR SEQUENCE FOR SECOND HALF

Work as for first half, but with the following exceptions.

Square 61: Poppy.

Square 72: Pink.

Square 74: Marigold.

Square 79: Mustard.

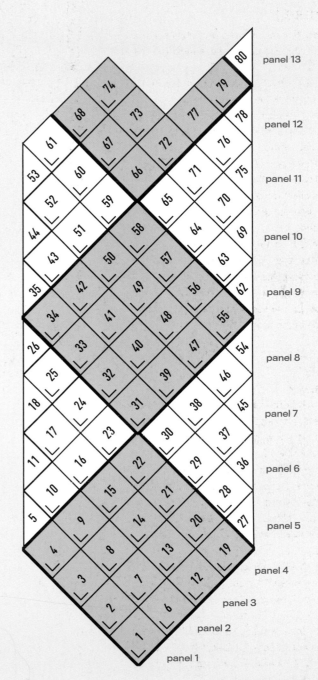

panel 13
panel 12
panel 11
panel 10
panel 9
panel 8
panel 7
panel 6
panel 5
panel 4
panel 3
panel 2
panel 1

Row 12: Change to Marigold. Sl 1 kwise, k8, sl 2 sts tog kwise, k1, p2sso, k8, p1—19 sts.
Row 14: Sl 1 kwise, k7, sl 2 sts tog kwise, k1, p2sso, k7, p1—17 sts.
Row 16: Change to Lady Slipper. Sl 1 kwise, k6, sl 2 sts tog kwise, k1, p2sso, k6, p1—15 sts.
Row 18: Sl 1 kwise, k5, sl 2 sts tog kwise, k1, p2sso, k5, p1—13 sts.
Row 20: Change to Marigold. Sl 1 kwise, k4, sl 2 sts tog kwise, k1, p2sso, k4, p1—11 sts.
Row 22: Sl 1 kwise, k3, sl 2 sts tog kwise, k1, p2sso, k3, p1—9 sts.
Row 24: Change to Lady Slipper. Sl 1 kwise, k2, sl 2 sts tog kwise, k1, p2sso, k2, p1—7 sts.
Row 26: Sl 1 kwise, k1, sl 2 sts tog kwise, k1, p2sso, k1, p1—5 sts.
Row 28: Sl 1 kwise, sl 2 sts tog kwise, k1, p2sso, p1—3 sts.
Row 30: Sl 2 sts tog kwise, k1, p2sso—1 st rem (**end st**). Cut yarn.
‹ *Square 2*
Knit the rem st of Square 1 with Seagreen and pull the Lady Slipper tail tight, **pick-knit** 15 sts along the upper edge of Square 1, go **"around the corner"** and pick-knit 1 st in the nearest CO loop, **turn work,** and K-CO 15 new sts—31 sts total. Work as for Square 1, but with Seagreen and Cornsilk and beg the first row with sl 1 pwise wyf.
‹ *Square 3*
Work as for Square 2 but with Pink and Gold.
‹ *Square 4*
Work as for Square 2 but with Lime and Periwinkle.
‹ *Left Triangle 5*
With Marigold, knit the end st from Square 4, pick-knit 14 sts along the upper edge of Square 4 and 1 st "around the corner"—16 sts total.

Row 1: (WS) Sl 1 pwise with yarn in front (wyf), purl to end.
Row 2: (RS) Sl 1 kwise, knit to the last 3 sts, **k2tog,** p1—15 sts.
Row 3: Sl 1 kwise, purl to end.
Row 4: Change to Lady Slipper. Sl 1 kwise, knit to the last 3 sts, k2tog, p1—14 sts. Rep Rows 3 and 4 until 4 sts rem, changing colors every 4 rows and ending with a WS row.
Next row: (RS) Sl 1 kwise, k2tog, p1—3 sts.
Next row: Sl 1 kwise, p2.
Next row: Sl 1 kwise, k2tog—2 sts.
Next row: Sl 1 pwise wyf, p1.
Next row: *Sl 1 kwise, k1, psso*—1 st rem. Pull the end st loose, cut the yarn, and thread the tail through it.

PANEL 2
‹ *Square 6*
With Poppy, K-CO 15 sts, place the needle in your right hand (i.e., turn work) and Panel 1 in your left hand, pick-knit 1 st "around the corner" *under* Square 1 in the far right CO loop, then pick-knit 15 sts along the right edge of Square 1—31 sts total. Work as for Square 1 but with Poppy and Mustard.
‹ *Square 7*
With Lilac, knit the end st of Square 6, pick-knit 14 sts along the upper edge of Square 6, 1 st in the upper tip of Square 1 and 15 sts along Square 2—31 sts total. Work as for Square 1 but with Lilac and Grass.
‹ *Squares 8 and 9*
Foll the sequence and colors indicated, work as for Square 7.
‹ *Square 10*
Work as for Square 9 using Mustard and Poppy, but do not pick-knit the last st into

the end of Triangle 5; pick-knit into the loop right before the end st.
‹ *Left Triangle 11*
Work as for Left Triangle 5, using Grass and Lilac, but when pick-knitting along Square 10, pick-knit the last st into the end st of Triangle 5.

PANEL 3
‹ *Squares 12 to 17*
Foll the sequence and colors indicated, work as for Panel 2.
‹ *Left Triangle 18*
Work as for Left Triangle 11 using colors indicated on page 17, but when pick-knitting along Square 17, pick-knit the last st into the end st of Triangle 11.

PANEL 4
‹ *Squares 19 to 25*
Foll the sequence and colors indicated, work as for Panel 2.
‹ *Left Triangle 26*
Work as for Left Triangle 18 using colors indicated on chart and pick-knit along Square 25 but pick-knit the last st into the end-st of Triangle 19.

PANEL 5
‹ *Right Triangle 27*
With Marigold, pick-knit the first st "around the corner" *under* Square 19 in the far right CO loop and pick-knit 15 sts along the right-hand side of Square 19—16 sts total.
Row 1: (WS) Sl 1 pwise wyf, purl to end.
Row 2: (RS) Sl 1 kwise, sl 1 more st kwise, k1, psso, knit to the last st, p1—15 sts.
Row 3: Sl 1 kwise, purl to end.
Row 4: Change to Lady Slipper. Sl 1 kwise, sl 1 more st kwise, k1, psso, knit to the last st, p1—14 sts.

Rep Rows 3 and 4 until 4 sts rem, changing colors every 4 rows and ending with a WS row.

Next row: (RS) Sl 1 kwise, sl 1 more st kwise, k1, psso, p1—3 sts.

Next row: Sl 1 kwise, p2.

Next row: Sl 1 kwise, sl 1 more st kwise, k1, psso—2 sts.

Next row: Sl 1 pwise, p1.

Next row: Sl 1 kwise, k1, psso—1 st rem. Leave the end st for the next right triangle (Triangle 36). When the next square (Square 28) of this panel is worked, pick-knit the first st into the edge st right next to the end st. Complete Squares 29 and 30 with colors indicated. Work Squares 31 to 34, repeating the colors as used in Squares 1 to 4. For Triangle 35, rep colors used in Triangle 5.

PANELS 6 TO 13

Cont as established, working squares and triangles in numerical order as indicated in the chart and foll the colors indicated, ending with Right Triangle 80, and working the single-color squares in garter st as foll:

Row 1: (WS) Sl 1 pwise wyf, knit to the last st, p1 (edge st).

Row 2: (RS) Sl 1 kwise (edge st), knit to 1 st before the center st (i.e., k13), **sl 1 kwise, k2tog, psso,** knit to last st (i.e., k13), p1 (edge st)—29 sts.

Row 3: Sl 1 kwise, knit to the last st, p1.

Row 4: Sl 1 kwise, knit to 1 st before the center st, sl 1 kwise, k2tog, psso, knit to the last st, p1—2 sts decreased.

Rep Rows 3 and 4 (working 1 fewer st before and after the center st) until 3 sts rem on a RS row.

Next row: (WS) Sl 1 kwise, k1, p1.

Next row: Sl 1 kwise, k2tog, psso—1 st (end st) rem.

SECOND HALF

Foll the sequence and colors indicated, work as for the first half.

FINISHING

Place the two halves together, so that the points of one half fit into the notches of the other. With yarn threaded on a tapestry needle, use the **mattress stitch** to sew the pieces together. **Weave in loose ends.**

EDGE

With Iris, pick-knit around the edge using several circular needles as necessary to accommodate all the sts: 22 sts along each triangle, 15 sts along each square, 1 st in each of the two points, and 1 st in each of the four corners—920 sts total. Place marker (pm) and join for working in rnds. Work k1, p1 rib for 4 rnds, inc in each rnd as foll: work **k1f&b** (or **p1f&b** if the st is purl) before and after each corner st (the corner sts are located at the lower edges of Triangles 5 and 27 at each end of the stole), maintain the established rib patt, working the new sts into the rib patt when possible. On round 4 only, k1f&b (or p1f&b) each side of the end st at both ends of stole (located at the lower point of each Square 1). **BO** all sts in pattern.

TASSELS (MAKE 2)

With Pink make **tassels** around a 4" (10 cm) wide cardboard, wrapped 40 times around. Sew one tassel to each pointed end.

join two blocks into a rectangle

Once you know how to make a block, it's a simple matter to join blocks together and/or to add squares to blocks to make large two-dimensional projects. Whether you're working with blocks or individual squares, the principle is the same. Just as squares can be worked one on another, entire blocks can be joined side by side. For example, let's see how two nine-square blocks can be joined along one side. For the example shown here, each square begins with 25 stitches and is worked in garter stitch. Different colors are used here so the individual squares are easy to see.

BLOCK 1

Knit and join squares as described on page 10, working 3 squares each in 3 panels: Squares 1, 2, and 3 for Panel 1; Squares 4, 5, and 6 for Panel 2; and Squares 7, 8, and 9 for Panel 3, working each square in a solid color.

BLOCK 2

So that the orientation of the squares in Block 2 is different than Block 1, rotate Block 1 counterclockwise 90 degrees so that Panel 3 is at the top. Work 3 panels of 3 squares each for Block 2 along the right edge of Block 1 as follows.

PANEL 1

‹ *Square 10*

K-CO 13 sts, place the needle in your right hand and Block 1 in your left hand (i.e., ***turn work***), then **pick-knit** 12 sts along the right edge of Square 1 (1 st in each CO-loop)—25 sts total.

Row 1: (WS) Sl 1 pwise with yarn in front (wyf), knit to the last st, p1 (***edge st***).

Row 2: (RS) Sl 1 kwise (edge st), k10, ***sl 1 kwise, k2tog, psso,*** k10, p1 (edge st)—23 sts.

Row 3: Sl 1 kwise, knit to the last st, p1.

Row 4: Sl 1 kwise, knit to 1 st before the center st (i.e., k9), sl 1 kwise, k2tog, psso, knit to the last st (i.e., k9), p1—21 sts.

Row 5: Sl 1 kwise, knit to the last st, p1.

Rep Rows 4 and 5 until 3 sts rem on a RS row.

Next row: (WS) Sl 1 kwise, k1, p1.

Next row: Sl 1 kwise, k2tog, psso—1 st rem (***end st***). This st becomes the first st of the next square.

‹ Square 11

This square will fill the notch between Squares 10, 1, and 4. With the needle holding the end st from Square 10, pick-knit 11 sts along the upper edge of Square 10 (12 sts on needle), 1 st between Squares 1 and 4, and 12 sts along the right edge of Square 4 (1 st in each CO-loop)—25 sts total. Work as for Square 10—1 st rem.

‹ Square 12

With the needle holding the end st of Square 11, pick-knit 11 sts along the upper edge of Square 11 (12 sts on needle), 1 st between Squares 4 and 7, and 12 sts along the right edge of Square 7—25 sts total. Work as for Square 10, but cut the yarn after the end st, pull this st loose, and pull the tail through it.

PANEL 2

‹ Square 13

K-CO 12 sts, then pick-knit 1 st **"around the corner"** *under* the lower right corner of Square 10, and 12 sts along the right edge of Square 10 (1 st in each edge st)—25 sts total. Work as for Square 10.

‹ Square 14

With the needle holding the end st of Square 13, pick-knit 11 st along the upper edge of Square 13 (12 sts on needle), 1 st in the tip of Square 10, and 12 sts along the right edge of Square 11—25 sts total. Work as for Square 10.

‹ Square 15

With the needle holding the end st of Square 14, pick 11 sts along the upper edge of Square 14 (12 sts on needle) 1 st in the tip of Square 11, 11 sts along the right edge of Square 12, and 1 st in the end st of Square 12 (pull the end-st tail tight to secure this st)—25 sts total. Work as for Square 12.

PANEL 3

‹ Squares 16, 17, and 18

Work as for Squares 13, 14, and 15, pick-knitting sts along right edge of Squares 13, 14, and 15, respectively.

pyramid pillow

This unusual pillow is constructed from two sixty-four-square blocks—each block made up of eight panels of eight squares each—that are joined along one side. The squares are worked checkerboard fashion, alternating solid black squares with striped black-and-white squares. The last few rows of some striped squares are worked in bright contrasting color for added visual interest. The blocks are sewn together along the remaining three sides to form a rhomboid shape. It is stuffed with a down pillow that has been sewn into the same rhomboid shape.

[materials]

FINISHED SIZE About 20½" (52 cm) wide and 20½" (52 cm) high.

YARN Fingering weight (#1 Super Fine) in 5 colors.

Shown here: Harrisville New England Knitter's Shetland (100% wool; 197 yd [180 m]/50 g): Black, 5 skeins; White, 2 skeins; Magenta, Red, and Poppy, 1 skein each.

NEEDLES Size 3 mm (between U.S. size 2 and 3): domino needles (page 6). Adjust needle size if necessary to obtain the correct gauge.

NOTIONS Tapestry needle; 24" (61 cm) square pillow.

GAUGE 1 square measures 2½" (6.5 cm) by 2½" (6.5 cm).

[techniques]

- knit squares and blocks (page 9)
- reading charts (page 10)
- join two blocks into a rectangle (page 20)
- weave in tails as you knit (page 12)
- see Glossary (page 133) for abbreviations and highlighted terms

[notes]

▸ To make a three-dimensional model of the cushion, make a photocopy of the two charts, cut them out, and tape them together so that Panel 1 of Block 2 (Squares 65 to 72) is attached to the base of Block 1 (Squares 1, 9, 17, 25, 33, 41, 49, and 57); Panel 8 of Block 2 (Squares 121 to 128) is at-tached to the top of Block 1 (Squares 8, 16, 24, 32, 40, 48, 56, and 64) to form a ring; Panel 1 of Block 1 (Squares 1 to 8) is attached to the base of Block 2 (Squares 65, 73, 81, 89, 97, 105, 113, and 121). Join the remaining 2 sides so that squares 60, 59, 58, 57, 72, 80, 88, and 96 attach to squares 61, 62, 63, 64, 128, 120, 112, and 104.

▸ Work the squares in numerical order in the colors specified (indicated by letters) on the chart. The direction of the numbers on the chart indicates the knitting direction.

▸ Each square is worked in garter stitch. Squares are worked in one color or two colors that alternate every two rows, others have a smaller section worked in a contrast color. See the chart for the color combinations.

COLOR KEY

Work the squares according to the foll color sequences.

A: K-CO/pick-knit and work entire square with Black.

B: K-CO/pick-knit sts and work 1 row with Black, then alternate 2 rows each of White and Black.

C: K-CO/pick-knit and work 1 row with Black, then alternate 2 rows each of White and Black until there are 6 ridges of Black and 5 ridges of White (21 rows total), then work to end of square with Magenta.

D: K-CO/pick-knit and work 1 row with Black, then alternate 2 rows each of White and Black until there are 6 ridges of Black and 5 ridges of White (21 rows total), then work to end of square with Red.

E: K-CO/pick-knit and work 1 row with Black, then alternate 2 rows each of White and Black until there are 6 ridges of Black and 5 ridges of White (21 rows total), then work to end of square with Poppy.

block 1

panel 1	panel 2	panel 3	panel 4	panel 5	panel 6	panel 7	panel 8
8/B	16/A	24/B	32/A	40/B	48/A	56/B	64/A
7/A	15/C	23/A	31/B	39/A	47/B	55/A	63/B
6/B	14/A	22/B	30/A	38/B	46/A	54/D	62/A
5/A	13/B	21/A	29/E	37/A	45/B	53/A	61/B
4/B	12/A	20/B	28/A	36/B	44/A	52/B	60/A
3/A	11/B	19/A	27/B	35/A	43/C	51/A	59/B
2/B	10/A	18/D	26/A	34/B	42/A	50/B	58/A
1/A	9/B	17/A	25/B	33/A	41/B	49/A	57/B

BLOCK 1

PANEL 1

< Square 1

With Black, **K-CO** 33 sts. Work in garter st as foll:

Row 1: (WS) Knit to the last st, p1.

Row 2: (RS) Sl 1 kwise (**edge st**), knit to 1 st before marked center st (i.e., k14), **sl 1 kwise, k2tog, psso,** knit to last sl (i.e., k14), p1 (edge st)—31 sts.

Row 3: Sl 1 kwise, knit to last st, p1.

Row 4: Sl 1 kwise, knit to 1 st before center st, sl 1 kwise, k2tog, psso, kni t to the last st, p1—2 sts decreased.

Row 5: Sl 1 kwise, knit to last st, p1. Rep Rows 4 and 5 until 3 sts rem on a RS row.

Next row: (WS) Sl 1 kwise, k1, p1.

Next row: (RS) Sl 1 kwise, k2tog, psso—1 st rem (**end st**).

< Square 2

Using the end st from Square 1 as the first st of Square 2, with Black, **pick-knit** 15 more sts along the upper edge of Square 1 (**Note:** Skip the first edge st because the end st from Square 1 is now the first st of Square 2), go **"around the corner"** and pick-knit 1 st in the outermost CO loop, **turn work,** and K-CO 16 new sts—33 sts total.

Row 1: (WS) Sl 2 pwise with yarn in front

block 2

panel 1	panel 2	panel 3	panel 4	panel 5	panel 6	panel 7	panel 8
72/A	80/B	88/A	96/B	104/A	112/B	120/A	128/B
71/B	79/A	87/E	95/A	103/B	111/A	119/B	127/A
70/A	78/B	86/A	94/B	102/A	110/D	118/A	126/D
69/E	77/A	85/B	93/A	101/B	109/A	117/B	125/A
68/A	76/B	84/A	92/C	100/A	108/C	116/A	124/B
67/B	75/A	83/B	91/A	99/B	107/A	115/E	123/A
66/A	74/C	82/A	90/B	98/A	106/B	114/A	122/B
65/B	73/A	81/B	89/A	97/B	105/A	113/B	121/A

Legend:
- Black
- White
- Magenta
- Red
- Poppy

square will be a different color in some squares; go ahead and use it as the first st of the new square, the stitch will be hidden as work progresses), and end the last st of the last square by pulling the end st loose, cutting the yarn, and threading the tail through it.

PANEL 2

< Square 9

With Black, K-CO 16 sts, place the needle in your right hand and Panel 1 in your left hand, then pick-knit 1 st "around the corner" *under* Square 1 in the outermost CO-loop, and 16 sts along the right edge of Square 1—33 sts total. Work as for Square 2, alternating between Black and White every 2nd row.

< Square 10

Using the end st from Square 9 as the first st of Square 10, pick-knit 15 sts along the upper edge of Square 9, 1 st into the tip of Square 1, and 16 sts along the right edge of Square 2—33 sts. Work as for Square 1.

< Squares 11 to 14

Foll the sequence and colors indicated on the chart, work as for Square 9, always beg at the top of the square just completed and the side of the corresponding square of the previous panel.

< Square 15

Work as for Square 11 until there are 6 black stripes (ridges) and 5 white stripes. After completing the 6th black stripe, join Magenta on next RS row and complete square in established patt.

< Square 16

Work as for Square 10, but pick-knit the last st in the end st of Square 8, work all rows in black, and end by pulling the end st loose, cutting the yarn, and threading the tail through it.

(wyf), knit to the last st, p1.

Row 2: (RS) Change to White, sl 1 kwise (edge st), knit to 1 st before the center st, sl 1 kwise, k2tog, psso, knit to last st, p1 (edge st)—31 sts.

Row 3 and all odd-numbered rows: Sl 1 kwise, knit to last st, p1.

Row 4: Change to Black, sl 1 kwise, knit to 1 st before the center st, sl 1 kwise, k2tog, psso, knit to the last st, p1—29 sts.

Row 6: Change to White, sl 1 kwise, knit to 1 st before the center st, sl 1 kwise, k2tog, psso, knit to the last st, p1—27 sts.

Row 8: Change to Black, rep Row 4—25 sts.

Row 10: Change to White, rep Row 4—23 sts. Cont changing colors between Black and White every other row, work in established patt until 3 sts rem on RS row.

Next row: (WS) Sl 1 kwise, k1, p1.

Next row: (RS) Sl 1 kwise, k2tog, psso—1 st rem (end st)

< Squares 3 to 8

Work as for Square 2 but foll the sequence and colors indicated on the chart, pick-knitting sts for each square from the top of the previous square (the end st of previous

PANELS 3 TO 8

Foll the sequence and colors indicated on the chart, work stitch patt as for Panel 2, inserting a third color (same as Square 15) in Squares 18 (Red), 29 (Poppy), 43 (Magenta), and 54 (Red). **BO** the end st of Square 64.

BLOCK 2

Rotate Block 1 so that Panel 8 (Squares 64, 63, 62, 61, 60, 59, 58, 57) is at the top. Work Block 2 to the right of Block 1, connecting it to Squares 1, 9, 17, 25, 33, 41, 49, and 57, as follows.

PANEL 1

‹ *Square 65*

With Black, K-CO 16 sts, place the needle in your right hand and Block 1 in your left hand, then pick-knit 1 st in the lower right corner of Square 1 and 16 sts along the right edge of Square 1—33 sts total. Work as for Square 2, but sl the first st pwise wyf and alternate between Black and White every 2nd row.

‹ *Square 66*

With Black, pick-knit 15 sts along the top of Square 65 (16 sts on needle), 1 st in the upper corner of Square 1, and 16 sts along the side of Square 9—33 sts total. Work as for for Square 1.

‹ *Squares 67 to 72*

Foll the sequence and colors specified on the chart, work as for Square 66, pick-knitting sts along the top of the previously worked square and along the side of the corresponding square of Block 1. Add a third color in Square 69 (Poppy). End Square 72 by pulling the end st loose, cutting the yarn, and threading the tail through it.

PANELS 2 TO 8

Foll the sequence and colors specified on the chart, work as for Panel 2 of Block 1, inserting a third color in Squares 74 (Magenta), 87 (Poppy), 92 (Magenta), 110 (Red), 115 (Poppy), and 126 (Red). BO the end of Square 128.

FINISHING

Weave in loose ends.

PILLOW INSERT

Carefully cut open one seam of a down pillow, then following the illustrations at right, sew the seam in the opposite direction to form a trapazoid. Set aside.

ASSEMBLY

With black threaded on a tapestry needle, use a *mattress stitch* to sew Panel 8 of Block 2 (Squares 121 to 128) to Squares 8, 16, 24, 32, 40, 48, 56, 64 of Block 1 to form a ring. Sew Panel 8 of Block 1 (Squares 57 to 64) to Squares 72, 80, 88, 96, 104, 112, 120 and 128 of Block 2 to form a bag. Place the pillow insert inside the bag, fold the remaining two sides together so that Squares 97, 105, 113, 121, 8, 7, 6, and 5 meet Squares 89, 81, 73, 65, 1, 2, 3, and 4. Sew together.

cut open one seam

bring the opposite sides together

sew seam to form trapezoid

chapter two
join two blocks into a pouch

Join two blocks (or squares) along two sides to form a pouch that can be basis for a hat, purse, backpack, or slippers! The sample blocks shown here consist of nine squares (three panels of three squares each). Each square begins with 25 stitches and is worked in garter stitch. Different colors are used here so the individual squares are easy to see.

BLOCK 1

Knit and join squares as described on page 10, working 3 squares each in 3 panels: Squares 1, 2, and 3 for Panel 1; Squares 4, 5, and 6 for Panel 2; and Squares 7, 8, and 9 for Panel 3, working each square in a solid color.

BLOCK 2

This block is worked onto Block 1 in such a way that when completed, the wrong side of Block 2 faces the wrong side of Block 1. To begin, rotate Block 1 so that the cast-on edge of Square 1 is at the top of the block. Stitches for the first square of Block 2 (Square 10) will be picked up along the cast-on edge of Square 1.

PANEL 1
‹ Square 10

With RS of Square 1 facing and working from right to left, **pick-knit** 1 st in each CO loop along right edge of Square 1 (from X to Z in the photograph), 1 st in the center point (Z), and 12 sts along the left edge (from Z to Y)—25 sts total.

Row 1: (WS) Sl 1 pwise with yarn in front (wyf), knit to the last st, p1 (**edge st**).
Row 2: (RS) Sl 1 kwise, k10, **sl 1 kwise, k2tog, psso,** k10, p1 (edge st)—23 sts.
Row 3: Sl 1 kwise, knit to the last st, p1.
Row 4: Sl 1 kwise, knit to 1 st before the center st (i.e., k9), sl 1 kwise, k2tog, psso, knit to the last st (i.e., k9), p1—21 sts.
Row 5: Sl 1 kwise, knit to the last st, p1.
Rep Rows 4 and 5 until 3 sts rem on a RS row.
Next row: (WS) Sl 1 kwise, k1, p1.
Next row: Sl 1 kwise, k2tog, psso—1 st rem (**end st**). Leave this st on the needle. Fold Square 10 over the top of Square 1 with WS tog so the pick-knit sts are on the inside.

‹ Square 11

Rotate the block clockwise so that Squares 7, 8, and 9 are at the top. Using the end st from Square 10 as the first st of Square 11, pick-knit 11 sts along the upper edge of Square 10 (12 sts on needle), turn work so RS of Block 1 is facing and pick-knit 1 st between Square 1 and Square 4, then 12 sts along the right edge of Square 4 (1 st in each CO loop). Work as for Square 10—1 st rem.

‹ Square 12

Using the end st from Square 11 as the first st of Square 12, pick-knit 11 more sts along the upper edge of Square 11 (12 sts on needle), turn work, pick-knit 1 st between Square 4 and Square 7, then 12 sts along the edge of Square 7 (1 st in each CO loop). Work as for Square 10 but cut the yarn after working the end st, pull this st loose, and pull the tail through it.

PANEL 2

‹ Square 13

Rotate Block 1 so that Squares 1, 2, and 3 are at the top. With RS facing and working from right to left, pick-knit 12 sts in the CO loops along Square 2, 1 st between Square 2 and Square 1, and 12 sts along the right edge of Square 10 (1 st in each edge st)—25 sts total. Work as for Square 10, but sl the first st pwise with yarn in front (wyf)—1 st rem.

‹ Square 14

Using the end st from Square 13 as the first st of Square 14, pick-knit 11 sts along the upper edge of Square 13 (12 sts on needle), 1 st in the tip of Square 10, and 12 sts along the right edge of Square 11 (1 st in each edge st)—25 sts total. Work as for Square 10, but sl the first st pwise wyf—1 st rem.

‹ Square 15

Using the end st from Square 14 as the first st of Square 15, pick-knit 11 sts along the upper edge of Square 14 (12 sts on needle), 1 st in the tip of Square 11, 11 sts along the right edge of Square 12 (1 st in each edge st), and 1 st in the end st of Square 12 (pull the tail tight to secure the st)—25 sts total. Work as for Square 10 but end by pulling the end st loose, cutting the yarn, and threading the tail through it.

<< Square 17

Using the end st from square 16 as the first st of Square 17, pick-knit 11 sts along the upper edge of Square 16 (12 sts on needle), 1 st in the tip of Square 13, and 12 sts along the right edge of Square 14 (1 st in each edge st)—25 sts total. Work as for Square 10 but sl the first st pwise wyf—1 st rem.

< Square 18

Using the end st from Square 17 as the first st of Square 18, pick-knit 11 sts along the upper edge of Square 17 (12 sts on needle), 1 st in the tip of Square 14, 11 sts along the right edge of Square 15, and 1 st in the end st of Square 15—25 sts total. Work as for Square 10 but BO the end st.

PANEL 3

< Square 16

Rotate Block 1 so that Squares 1, 2, and 3 are at the top. With RS facing and working from right to left, pick-knit 12 sts in the CO loops along Square 3, 1 st between Square 3 and Square 2, turn again, and pick-knit 12 sts along the the right edge of Square 13 (1 st in each edge st)—25 sts total. Work as for Square 10 but sl the first st pwise wyf—1 st rem.

two-block hat

This hat shows how easy it is to join blocks together to make a three-dimensional piece. This well-fitting hat begins with two nine-square blocks (each consisting of three panels of three squares each) joined along two sides to form the top of the hat, then two more blocks are joined in the notches between the first two blocks to fill in the gaps and form triangular "earflaps." A knitted-on garter-stitch edging finishes off the raw edges of the blocks and ends in straps that tie under the chin.

[materials]

FINISHED SIZE About 14" (35.5 cm) in circumference; stretches to fit head circumferences of about 18" to 20" (45.5 to 51 cm). To fit 2–4 years.

YARN Fingering weight (#1 Super Fine) in 3 colors.

Shown here: Dale of Norway Baby Ull (100% superwash wool; 191 yd [175 m]/50 g): #5545 Deep Blue, #8216 Light Green; #5914 Bright Blue, 1 skein each.

NEEDLES Size U.S. 1 or 2 (2.5 mm): domino needles (page 6) and 16" (40 cm) circular (cir). Adjust needle size if necessary to obtain the correct gauge.

NOTIONS Marker (m); tapestry needle; stitch holder.

GAUGE 1 square measures 4 by 4 cm (1.6" by 1.6") and 6 cm (2.4") across the diagonal.

[techniques]

▾ knit squares and blocks (page 9)
▾ reading charts (page 10)
▾ join two blocks into a pouch (page 30)
▾ weave in tails as you knit (page 12)
▾ see Glossary (page 133) for abbreviations and highlighted terms

[notes]

▾ The hat is worked from the top down.
▾ To make the hat smaller or bigger, decrease or increase the number of stitches in each square.
▾ To make a three-dimensional model of the hat, make a photocopy of the chart, cut it out, and tape it together connecting Squares 28, 31, and 34 to Squares 3, 6, and 9.

- Work the squares in numerical order in the colors specified (indicated by letters) on the chart. The direction of the numbers on the chart indicates the knitting direction.
- Each square is worked in garter stitch in two colors that alternate every four rows. See the chart for the color combinations.

BLOCK 1
PANEL 1
‹ *Square 1*

With Deep Blue, **K-CO** 23 sts. Work in garter-stitch stripes, changing colors every 4th row as foll:

Row 1: (WS) Knit to the last st, p1.
Row 2: (RS) Sl 1 kwise (**edge st**), knit to 1 st before the center st (i.e., k9), **sl 1 kwise, k2tog, psso,** k9, p1 (edge st)—2 sts decreased, 21 sts.
Row 3: Sl 1 kwise (edge st), knit to last st, p1 (edge st).
Row 4: Change to Green. Sl 1 kwise, knit to 1 st before the center st (i.e., k8), sl 1 kwise, k2tog, psso, knit to the last st (i.e., k8), p1—19 sts.
Row 5: Sl 1 kwise, knit to last st, p1.
Rep Rows 4 and 5, changing colors every 4th row until 3 sts rem on a RS row.
Next row: (WS) Sl 1 kwise, k1, p1.
Next row: (RS) Sl 1 kwise, k2tog, psso—1 st rem (**end st**).

‹ *Square 2*

Using the end st from Square 1 as the first st of Square 2, with Deep Blue, **pick-knit** 10 more sts along the upper edge of Square 1 (*Note:* Skip the first edge st because the end st from Square 1 is now the first st of Square 2; on some squares

the first st may be a different color, but it doesn't matter because it will be hidden by subsequent work), go **"around the corner"** and pick-knit 1 st in the nearest CO loop, **turn work,** and K-CO 11 new sts—23 sts total.

Row 1: (WS) Knit to last st, p1. Cont as for Square 1, changing between Deep Blue and Bright Blue every 4th row.

‹ *Square 3*

With the colors specified on the chart, work as for Square 2, pick-knitting sts at the top of Square 2 and end by pulling the end st loose, cutting the yarn, and threading the tail through it.

PANEL 2
‹ *Square 4*

With Deep Blue, K-CO 11 sts, pick-knit 1 st "around the corner" *under* Square 1 in the far right CO loop, then pick-knit 11 sts along the right edge of Square 1—23 sts total. Work as for Square 1 but beg the first row with sl 1 pwise with yarn in front (wyf), alternating between Deep Blue and Bright Blue every 4th row.

‹ *Square 5*

Foll the sequence and colors indicated on the chart, work as for Square 2, beginning at the top of the square just completed and the side of the corresponding square of the previous panel.

‹ *Square 6*

Foll the sequence and colors indicated on the chart, work as for Square 5 but pick-knit the last st in the end st of Square 3, and end by pulling the end st loose, cutting the yarn, and threading the tail through it.

PANEL 3

Foll the sequence and colors indicated on the chart, work Squares 7, 8, and 9 as for Squares 4, 5, and 6 of Panel 2. BO the end st of Square 9.

BLOCK 2

Rotate Block 1 so that the 31 CO sts of Square 1 are at the top of Block 1. Work Block 2 along the side of Block 1 to form a pouch as follows.

PANEL 1
‹ *Square 10*

With Deep Blue, RS facing, and working from right to left, pick-knit 1 st in each CO loop along right edge of Square 1, 1 st in

COLOR KEY

A: K-CO or pick-knit and knit 3 rows of Deep Blue, then alternate 4 rows each of Light Green and Deep Blue.

B: K-CO or pick-knit and knit 3 rows of Deep Blue, then alternate 4 rows each of Bright Blue and Deep Blue.

C: K-CO or pick-knit and knit 3 rows of Bright Blue, then alternate 4 rows each of Light Green and Bright Blue.

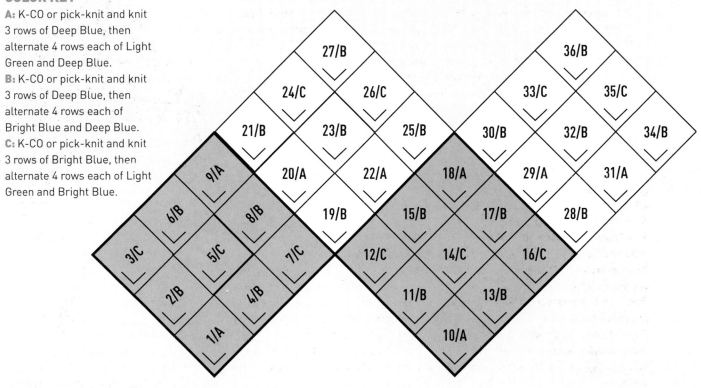

the point, and 11 sts along the left edge—23 sts total.

Row 1: (WS) Sl 1 pwise wyf (edge st), knit to the last st, p1 (edge st).

Row 2: (RS) Sl 1 kwise, k9, sl 1 kwise, k2tog, psso, k9, p1—21 sts.

Row 3: Sl 1 kwise, knit to the last st, p1.

Row 4: Change to Light Green. Sl 1 kwise, knit to 1 st before the center st (i.e., k8), sl 1 kwise, k2tog, psso, knit to the last st

(i.e., k8), p1—19 sts.

Row 5: Sl 1 kwise, knit to the last st, p1. Rep Rows 4 and 5, changing between Light Green and Deep Blue every 4th row until 3 sts rem on a RS row.

Next row: (WS) Sl 1 kwise, k1, p1.

Next row: Sl 1 kwise, k2tog, psso—1 st rem (end st).

‹ *Square 11*

Rotate Square 10 clockwise so that

Squares 7, 8, and 9 are at the top. With RS facing, using the end st from Square 10 as the first st of Square 11, and working from right to left, pick-knit 10 sts along the upper edge of Square 10 (11 sts on needle), turn work so RS of Block 1 is facing and pick-knit 1 st between Square 1 and Square 4, and 11 sts along the right edge of Square 4 (1 st in each CO loop). Work as for Square 10.

‹ Square 12

With the colors specified on the chart, work as for Square 11, pick-knitting sts along the left edge of Square 11, between Squares 4 and 7, and along the right edge of Square 7, and ending by pulling the end st loose, cutting the yarn, and threading the tail through it.

PANEL 2
‹ Square 13

With Deep Blue, RS facing, and working from right to left, pick-knit 1 st in each CO loop along right edge of Square 2 of Block 1, 1 st between Square 2 and Square 1, and 11 sts along the right edge of Square 10 of Block 2—23 sts total. Work as for Square 1, alternating between Deep Blue and Bright Blue every 4th row.

‹ Square 14

With Bright Blue, RS facing, and working from right to left, pick-knit 1 st in each edge st along top edge of Square 13, 1 st in the tip of Square 10, and 11 sts along the right edge of Square 11—23 sts total. Work as for Square 1, alternating between Bright Blue and Light Green.

‹ Square 15

Foll the colors specified on the chart, work as for Square 14, pick-knitting sts along top edge of Square 14, the tip of Square 11, and the right edge of Square 12, and ending by pulling the end st loose, cutting the yarn, and threading the tail through it.

PANEL 3

Foll the sequence and colors indicated on the chart, work as for Panel 2, pick-knitting sts along the right edge of Panel 2. BO the end st of Square 18.

BLOCK 3
PANEL 1
‹ Square 19

With Deep Blue, RS facing, and working from right to left, pick-knit 1 st in each edge st along top edge of Square 12 (11 sts on needle), 1 st between Squares 12 and 7, and 11 sts along the edge of Square 7—23 sts total. Work as for Square 10, alternating between Deep Blue and Bright Blue every 4th row.

‹ Square 20

Foll the sequence and colors specified on the chart, pick-knit 11 sts along the upper edge of Square 19, 1 st between Squares 7 and 8, and 11 sts along the edge of Square 8. Work as for Square 11.

‹ *Square 21*

Work as for Square 20, but pick-knit sts along the upper edge of Square 20, 1 st between Squares 8 and 9, and 11 sts along the edge of Square 9. Work as for Square 1 but end by pulling the end st loose, cutting the yarn, and threading the tail through it.

PANELS 2 AND 3

Foll the sequence and colors specified on the chart, work Squares 22 to 27 as for Squares 13 to 18 of Block 2, pick-knitting sts for Square 22 along the top of Square 15 and pick-knitting sts for Square 25 along the top of Square 18. BO the end st of Square 27.

BLOCK 4

Foll the sequence and colors specified on the chart, and beg with Squares 18, 17, 16, 3, 6, and 9 at the top, work Squares 28 to 36 as for Squares 19 to 27 of Block 3, pick-knitting sts for Square 28 along the top of Squares 3 and 16; sts for Square 29 along Squares 28, 16, and 17; sts for Square 30 along Squares 29, 17, and 18; sts for Square 31 along the top of Square 6; and sts for Square 34 along the top of Square 9.

FINISHING

Weave in loose ends.

BACK NECK EDGING

With Deep Blue, cir needle, and RS facing, pick-knit 1 st in the tip of Square 36, 11 sts each along Squares 36, 33, and 30, 1 st in the tip of Square 18 (center back), 11 sts each along Squares 25, 26, and 27, and 1 st in the tip of Square 27—69 sts total. Knit 1 row. Cut yarn. Join Bright Blue and K-CO 5 new sts onto the same needle with the previous 69 sts—74 sts.

Row 1: (RS) K4, *p2tog* (1 Bright Blue and 1 Deep Blue st)—1 Deep Blue st decreased. Turn work.

Row 2: (WS) Sl 1 kwise, k3, p1.

Row 3: Sl 1 kwise, k3, p2tog. Turn work.

Rep Rows 2 and 3, and *at the same time* dec 5 sts as foll: work to the point where two squares are joined, then dec on RS row as foll: Sl 1 kwise, k3, *p3tog.* Cont in this manner until all Deep Blue sts have been decreased, ending with a WS row—5 Bright Blue sts. Do not BO.

FRONT EDGING AND STRAPS

Sl the 5 Bright Blue sts onto a holder. With Deep Blue, cir needle, and RS facing, pick-knit 1 st in the tip of Square 27, then 11 sts each along Squares 27, 24, and 21, 1 st in the tip of Square 9 (center front), 11 sts each along Squares 34, 35, and 36, and 1 st in the tip of Square 36—69 Deep Blue sts. With Deep Blue, knit 1 row across the 69 sts. Cut Deep Blue yarn. Slip the 5 Bright Blue sts from holder onto cir needle in front of the 69 Deep Blue sts and in position ready to knit—74 sts total. Set aside.

FIRST STRAP

With Bright Blue and domino needle, K-CO 5 sts. Cont as foll:

Row 1: K4, p1.

Row 2: Sl 1 kwise, k3, p1.

Rep Row 2 until piece measures 6¼" (16 cm) from CO. Place these 5 Bright Blue sts onto the cir needle holding 74 sts so that the 5 sts just worked for strap are ahead of the 5 Bright Blue sts already on the cir needle. Check carefully to make sure all pieces have their RS and WS in the same direction. Cont with Bright Blue as foll:

Row 1: Sl 1 kwise, k3, p2tog (this will join the last st of 5 Bright Blue strap sts with the first st of the second group of 5 Bright Blue sts). Turn work.

Row 2: Sl 1 kwise, k3, p1.

Rep Rows 1 and 2 until the second set of Bright Blue sts is joined to the first set, then cont rep Rows 1 and 2 attaching the Deep Blue sts to the Bright Blue sts in the same manner until all Deep Blue sts are attached and 5 Bright Blue sts. Do not BO.

SECOND STRAP

Cont with Bright Blue and 5 rem sts, work as foll:

Row 1: Sl 1 kwise, k3, p2tog (the last st of 5 and 1 K-CO loop from Back Neck Edging).

Row 2: Sl 1 kwise, k3, p1.

Rep Rows 1 and 2 until all 5 K-CO sts are joined to strap (10 rows). Cont strap as foll:

Row 1: Sl 1 kwise, k3, p1.

Rep Row 1 until strap length measures same as first strap. BO all sts.

Sew the gap between the edging and the strap on both sides.

heart purse

This purse is inspired by the braided paper hearts made famous by Hans Christian Andersen. Although the paper hearts are traditionally used as Christmas ornaments, this bright and cheerful bag is appropriate all year round. It is made from two thirty-six-square blocks (each consisting of six panels of six squares each) that are joined along two sides to form a "pocket." The squares are worked checkerboard fashion with colors alternating every square. The colors are reversed on the second block. Solid-colored garter-stitch bands form the upper edge. The handles are double-knitted bands; the button loop is a crocheted chain.

[materials]

FINISHED SIZE About 36" (91 cm) wide and 18" (45.5 cm) high before felting; about 31½" (80 cm) wide and 15¾" (40 cm) high, after felting.

YARN Fingering weight (#1 Super Fine) in 2 colors.

Shown here: Harrisville New England Knitter's Shetland (100% wool; 217 yd [200 m]/50 g): Poppy (A) and Magenta (B) 1 skein each.

NEEDLES Size U.S. 4 (3.5 mm): domino needles (page 6) and 24" (60 cm) circular (cir). Adjust needle size if necessary to obtain the correct gauge.

NOTIONS Tapestry needle; one 1" (2.5 cm) button; sharp-point sewing needle and matching thread; size U.S. C/2 (2.75 mm) crochet hook.

GAUGE Before felting: 1 square measures about 2¼" by 2¼" (5.6 by 5.6 cm); 1 block measures about 14" by 14" (34 by 34 cm). After felting: 1 square measures about 1¾" by 1¾" (4.8 by 4.8 cm); 1 block measures about 11¾" by 11¾" (30 by 30 cm).

[techniques]

▼ knit squares and blocks (page 9)
▼ reading charts (page 10)

▼ join two blocks into a pouch (page 30)
▼ weave in tails as you knit (page 12)
▼ see Glossary (page 133) for abbreviations and highlighted terms

[notes]

▼ The chart shows one block (the purse front) that consists of 6 panels of 6 squares each. Reverse the colors of the squares for the second block (the purse back).

▼ Work the squares in numerical order (indicated by number) in the colors specified (indicated by letters). The direction of the numbers on the chart indicates the knitting direction.

▼ The squares are worked alternately Magenta and Poppy in a checkerboard pattern.

▼ The top edge borders may require trimming after felting, to shorten or smooth out the BO edges, and provide a more defined edge. The borders on the project were trimmed slightly.

▼ Individual felting measurements may differ (see Felting, page 137.)

BLOCK 1 (Bag Front)
PANEL 1
‹ *Square 1*

With Magenta, **K-CO** 25 sts. Work in garter stitch as foll:

Row 1: (WS) Knit to the last st, p1 (**edge st**).

Row 2: (RS) Sl 1 kwise (edge st), knit to 1 st before the center st (i.e., k10), **sl 1 kwise, k2tog, psso,** knit to last st (i.e., k10), p1 (edge st).

Row 3: Sl 1 kwise, knit to last st, p1.

Row 4: Sl 1 kwise, knit to 1 st before the center st, sl 1 kwise, k2tog, psso, knit to the last st, p1—2 sts decreased.

Row 5: Sl 1 kwise, knit to last st, p1.

Rep Rows 4 and 5 until 3 sts rem on a RS row.

Next row: (WS) Sl 1 kwise, k1, p1.

Next row: (RS) Sl 1 kwise, k2tog, psso—1 st rem (**end st**).

‹ *Square 2*

Using the end st from Square 1 as the first st of Square 2, with Poppy, **pick-knit** 11 more sts along the upper edge of Square 1 (**Note:** Skip the first edge st because the end st from Square 1 is now the first st of Square 2; it doesn't matter that it's a different color), go **"around the corner"** and pick-knit 1 st in the nearest CO loop, **turn work,** and K-CO 12 new sts—25 sts total. Work as for Square 1.

‹ *Squares 3 to 6*

With colors specified on the chart, work as Square 2, always pick-knitting sts along the top of the square just completed. End Square 6 by pulling the end st loose, cutting the yarn, and threading the tail through it.

PANEL 2

‹ *Square 7*

With Poppy, K-CO 12 sts, place the needle in your right hand and pick-knit 1 st "around the corner" *under* Square 1 in the far right CO loop, then pick-knit 12 sts along the right edge of Square 1—25 sts total. Work as for Square 1 but beg the first row with sl 1 pwise with yarn in front (wyf).

‹ *Square 8*

With Magenta, knit the end st of Square 7, pick-knit 12 sts along the upper edge of Square 2, 1 st in the tip of Square 1, and 12 sts along Square 2—25 sts total. Work as for Square 1.

‹ *Squares 9 to 11*

Foll the sequence and colors indicated on the chart, work as for Square 8, always beg at the top of the square just completed.

‹ *Square 12*

Work as for Square 11, but pick-knit the last st in the end st of the last square of the panel just completed (Square 6). End by pulling the end st loose, cutting the yarn, and threading the tail through it.

PANELS 3 TO 6

Foll the sequence and colors indicated on the chart, work as for Panel 2. BO the end st of Square 36.

BLOCK 2 (Bag Back)

Rotate Block 1 so that Square 1 is at the top.

PANEL 1
‹ *Square 1*

With Poppy, RS facing, and working from right to left, pick-knit 1 st in each CO loop along the edge of Square 1, 1 st in the center point, and 12 sts along the left edge—25 sts total. Work as for Square 1, but beg the first row with sl 1 pwise wyf.

‹ *Square 2*

Using the end st from Square 1 as the first st of Square 2 and Magenta, pick-knit 11 sts along the upper edge of Square 1 (12 sts on needle), turn work so RS of Block 1 is facing and pick-knit 1 st between Square 1 and Square 7, then 12 sts along the edge of Square 7 (1 st in each CO loop). Work as for Square 1.

‹ *Squares 3 to 6*

Alternating colors for each square, work as for Square 2, always pick-knitting sts along the top of the square just completed and along the next available square of Block 1. End Square 6 by pulling the end st loose, cutting the yarn, and threading the tail through it.

PANEL 2
‹ *Square 7*

Rotate Block 1 so that Squares 1, 2, 3, 4, 5, and 6 are at the top. With Magenta, RS facing, and working from right to left, pick-knit 1 st in each CO loop along the edge of Square 2 of Block 1, 1 st between Squares 2 and 1 on Block 1 and 12 sts along the left edge of Square 1 of Block 2—25 sts total. Work as for Square 1 but beg the first row with sl 1 pwise wyf.

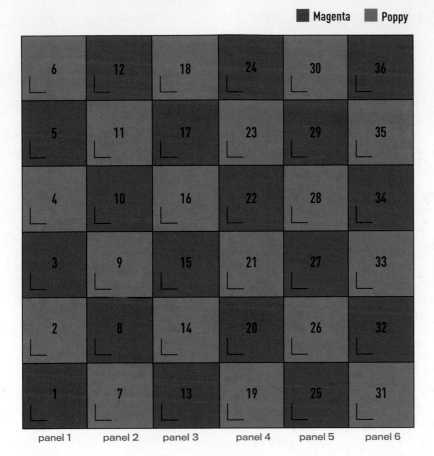

■ Magenta ■ Poppy

panel 1 panel 2 panel 3 panel 4 panel 5 panel 6

‹ Squares 8 to 12

Alternating colors for each square (reversing the colors on the chart), work as for Square 2, always pick-knitting sts along the top of the square just completed and along the next available square of Block 1, and BO all sts at the end of Square 6. When pick-knitting sts for Square 12, pick-knit the last st in the end st of Square 6. End Square 12 by pulling the end st loose, cutting the yarn, and threading the tail through it.

PANELS 3 TO 6

Foll the sequence and cont reversing the colors on the chart, work as for Panel 2, beg each panel by pick-knitting sts along squares of Block 1 and the right edge of the previous panel of Block 2. BO the end st of Square 36.

TOP EDGING
LEFT SIDE

With Magenta, RS facing, beg at the right (top) corner of Square 36 of Block 1, and working from right to left, pick-knit 12 sts along each square and 1 st between each square along the top of Block 1, then along the top of Block 2, ending at the far left (top) corner of Block 2—155 sts total.

Row 1: (WS) Sl 1 pwise wyf, knit to last st, p1.
Row 2: (RS) Sl 1 kwise, **ssk,** knit to 1 st before center st, sl 1 kwise, k2tog, psso, knit to the last 3 sts, **k2tog,** p1—4 sts decreased.
Row 3: Sl 1 kwise, knit to last st, p1.
Rep Rows 2 and 3, always working the decreases on the center 3 sts until 107 sts rem—13 garter ridges on RS. Work 1 WS row. With RS facing, BO all sts.

RIGHT SIDE

With Poppy, work as for Right Side Edge, pick-knitting sts along tops of rem squares.

FINISHING
Weave in loose ends.

HANDLES (MAKE 2)

With Poppy, CO 12 sts. Work a double-knitted band as foll: *K1, sl 1 pwise wyf; rep from *. Rep this row until piece measures about 15" (38 cm) long before felting (about 12" [30 cm] after felting). Trim the ends to shorten, if desired. With sharp-point sewing needle and matching thread, sew the handles onto the inside of the purse.

FELTING

Felt in the washing machine as described on page 137.

BUTTON LOOP

With Poppy and crochet hook, make a **crochet chain** about 4" (10 cm) long. Turn work 1 **slip st** in each chain. Fasten off. Fold chain in half to form a loop and secure each end to the WS of the center top of the purse back.

LINING

Using the bag as a template, cut 2 pieces of lining fabric along the bias. Sew the lining pieces tog, then sew into WS of bag so that RS of lining is visible inside the bag, and so that lining covers the ends of the handles and button loop.

Sew button to bag front opposite button loop.

backpack

This clever backpack is formed from two blocks (each consisting of three panels of three squares each) that are joined along two sides to make a "pocket" at the base of the bag. The gaps between the two foundation blocks are filled in with additional squares. To add length, additional squares are added in a circular manner. The upper edge is punctuated with triangles to form a straight border on half of the bag, while squares are continued to make a point for the fold-over flap on the other half. The squares are all knitted in black, then colorful dots of scrap yarns are added with needle felting.

[materials]

FINISHED SIZE About 27½" (70 cm) in circumference and 20½" (52 cm) long from tip to triangles across opening, before felting. About 24½" (62 cm) in circumference and 18¼" (46.5 cm) long, after felting.

YARN Fingering weight (#1 Super Fine).

Shown here: Harrisville New England Knitter's Shetland (100% wool; 217 yd [200 m]/50 g): Black, 4 skeins. Small amounts of Marigold, Gold, Lady Slipper, Pink, Poppy, and Red for embellishment.

NEEDLES Size U.S. 4 or 6 (3.5 or 4 mm): domino needles (page 6). Adjust needle size if necessary to obtain the correct gauge.

NOTIONS Tapestry needle; about ¾ yd (68.5 cm) woven fabric about 30" (76 cm) wide for lining; felting needle and mat (used here are Clover model 8900 and 8910, respectively); two snap hooks (Clover Swivel Ring 6195, 3 cm); two D-rings (shown here is Clover D-Ring 1 3/16 6183, 3 cm); 67" (170 cm) nylon webbing about 1¾" (4.5 cm) wide; one 1" (2.5 cm) button.

GAUGE Each square measures about 3¼" by 3¼" (8.2 by 8.2 cm), and 4½" (11.6 cm) on the diagonal, before felting; each square measures 3" by 3" (7.7 by 7.7 cm) and 4¾" (12 cm) on the diagonal, after felting.

[techniques]

▼ knit squares and blocks (page 9)
▼ reading charts (page 10)
▼ join two blocks into a pouch (page 30)
▼ weave in tails as you knit (page 12)
▼ see Glossary (page 133) for abbreviations and highlighted terms

[notes]

▼ To make a three-dimensional model of the backpack or belt bag, make a photocopy of the chart, cut it out, and tape it together so that Panel 1 of Block 2 is attached to the base of Block 1 (Squares 1, 4, and 7); Panel 1 of Block 1 is attached to the base of Block 2 (Squares 10, 13, and 16); and Squares 3, 24, and 31 fit into the notches between Squares 22, 30, and 42.

▼ Work the squares in garter stitch in numerical order in the colors specified (indicated by letters) on the chart. The direction of the numbers on the chart indicates the knitting direction.

▼ The rounds are indicated by numbers in the left side of the chart.

BLOCK 1
PANEL 1
‹ Square 1

With Black, **K-CO** 37 sts. Work in garter st as foll:

Row 1: (WS) Knit to the last st, p1 (**edge st**).
Row 2: (RS) Sl 1 kwise (edge st), knit to 1 st before center st (i.e., k16), **sl 1 kwise, k2tog, psso,** k16, p1 (edge st)—35 sts.
Row 3: Sl 1 kwise, knit to last st, p1.
Row 4: Sl 1 kwise, knit to 1 st before the center st (i.e., k15), sl 1 kwise, k2tog, psso, knit to the last st (i.e., k15), p1—33 sts.
Row 5: Sl 1 kwise, knit to last st, p1.
Rep Rows 4 and 5 until 3 sts rem on a RS row.
Next row: (WS) Sl 1 kwise, k1, p1.
Next row: (RS) Sl 1 kwise, k2tog, psso—1 st rem (**end st**).

‹ Square 2

Using the end st from Square 1 as the first st of Square 2, with Black, **pick-knit** 17 more sts along the upper edge of Square 1 (**Note:** Skip the first edge st because the end st from Square 1 is now the first st of Square 2), go **"around the corner"** and pick-knit 1 st in the nearest CO loop, **turn work,** and K-CO 18 new sts—37 sts total. Work as for Square 1.

‹ Square 3

Work as for Square 2, pick-knitting sts at the top of Square 2 and ending by pulling the end st loose, cutting the yarn, and threading the tail through it.

PANEL 2
‹ Square 4

K-CO 18 sts, place the needle in your right hand and pick-knit 1 st "around the corner" *under* Square 1 in the far right CO loop, and 18 sts along the right edge of Square 1—37 sts total. Work as for Square 1 but beg the first row with sl 1 pwise with yarn in front (wyf).

‹ Square 5

Foll the placement indicated on the chart, work as for Square 2, always beg at the top of the square just completed and the side of the corresponding square of the previous panel.

‹ Square 6

Work as for Square 5 but when pick-knitting sts, pick-knit the last st in the end st of Square 3 (pull the tail tight to secure the st). End by pulling the end st loose, cutting the yarn, and threading the tail through it.

PANEL 3

Foll the placement indicated on the chart, work Squares 7, 8, and 9 as for Squares 4, 5, and 6 of Panel 2. **BO** the end st of Square 9.

BLOCK 2

Rotate Block 1 so that Square 1 is at the top.

PANEL 1
‹ Square 10

With RS of Square 1 facing and working from right to left, pick-knit 18 sts (1 st in each CO loop) along Square 1, 1 st in the center point, and 18 sts (1 st in each CO loop) along the other edge of Square 1—37 sts total. Work as for Square 1 but beg the first row with sl 1 pwise wyf.

‹ Square 11

Using the end st from Square 10 as the first st of Square 11, pick-knit 17 sts along the upper edge of Square 10 (18 sts on needle), turn work so RS of Block 1 is facing and and pick-knit 1 st between Square 1 and Square 4, and 18 sts along the edge of Square 4 (1 st in each CO loop)—37 sts total. Work as for Square 1 but beg the first row with sl 1 pwise wyf.

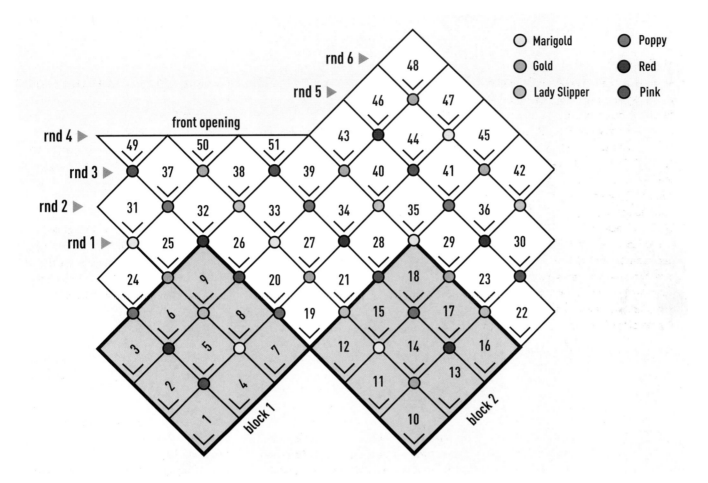

Legend:
- ○ Marigold
- ◔ Gold
- ◑ Lady Slipper
- ● Poppy
- ● Red
- ◕ Pink

< *Square 12*

Work as for Square 11, pick-knitting sts along the left edge of Square 11, 1 st between Squares 4 and 7, and along the right edge of Square 7. End by pulling the end st loose, cutting the yarn, and threading the tail through it.

PANEL 2

< *Square 13*

With RS of Block 1 facing and working from right to left, pick-knit 1 st in each of the 17 CO loops along edge of Square 2, 1 st between Squares 2 and 1, and 18 sts along the right edge of Square 10 of Block 2—37 sts total. Work as for Square 1 but begin the first row with sl 1 pwise wyf.

< *Square 14*

With RS facing and working from right to left, pick-knit 1 st in 17 sts along the upper edge of Square 13, 1 st in the tip of Square 10, and 18 sts along the right edge of Square 11—37 sts total. Work as for Square 1 but begin the first row with sl 1 pwise wyf.

‹ *Square 15*

Work as for Square 14 but when pick-knitting sts along top edge of Square 14 and side of Square 12, pick-knit the last st in the end st of the panel just completed (pull the tail tight to secure the st). End by pulling the end st loose, cutting the yarn, and threading the tail through it.

PANEL 3

Foll the placement specified on the chart, work Squares 16, 17, and 18 as for Panel 2 (Squares 13, 14, and 15), pick-knitting sts along the edge of Panel 2.

FILL IN THE NOTCHES

Fill in the notches between Block 1 and Block 2 by working additional squares as follows.

‹ *Square 19*

With RS facing and working from right to left, pick-knit 18 sts (1 in each edge st) along the edge of Square 12, 1 st between Squares 12 and 7, and 18 sts along the edge of Square 7—37 sts total. Work as for Square 1 but beg the first row with sl 1 pwise wyf.

‹ *Square 20*

With RS facing and working from right to left, pick-knit 17 sts along the upper edge of Square 19, 1 st at the tip of Square 7, and 18 sts along the edge of Square 8—37 sts total. Work as for Square 1 but beg the first row with sl 1 pwise wyf. BO the end st.

‹ *Square 21*

With RS facing and working from right to left, pick-knit 18 sts along the upper edge of Square 15, 1 st at the tip of Square 12, and 18 sts along the edge of Square 19—37 sts total. Work as for Square 1 but beg the first row with sl 1 pwise wyf. BO the end st.

‹ Square 22

With RS facing and working from right to left, pick-knit 18 sts along the upper edge of Square 3, 1 st between Squares 3 and 16, and 18 sts along the edge of Square 16—37 sts total. Work as for Square 1 but beg the first row with sl 1 pwise wyf.

‹ Square 23

With RS facing and working from right to left, pick-knit 17 sts along the edge of Square 22, 1 st at the tip of Square 16, and 18 sts along the edge of Square 17—37 sts total. Work as for Square 1 but beg the first row with sl 1 pwise wyf. BO the end st.

‹ Square 24

With RS facing and working from right to left, pick-knit 18 sts along top of Square 6, 1 st at the tip of Square 3, and 18 sts along the edge of Square 22—37 sts total. Work as for Square 1 but beg the first row with sl 1 pwise wyf. BO the end st.

ADD LENGTH

Add length to the bag by working additional squares in a series of rounds.

ROUND 1

‹ Squares 25 to 30

Foll the placement indicated on the chart, work each square as for Square 5 but BO the end st of each square.

ROUND 2

‹ Squares 31 to 36

Foll the placement indicated on the chart, work Squares 31 to 36 as for Round 1.

ROUND 3

‹ Squares 37 to 42

Foll the placement indicated on the chart, work Squares 37 to 42 as for Round 1.

ROUND 4

Work squares in three of the notches to begin the fold-over top and work triangles in the other three notches to form the top of the backpack as follows.

‹ Squares 43, 44, and 45

Foll the placement indicated on the chart, work as for Square 19.

‹ Triangle 49

With RS facing and working from right to left, pick-knit 18 sts (1 st in each edge st) along the upper edge of Square 37, 1 st at the tip of Square 31, and 18 sts along the right side of Block 42—37 sts total.

Row 1: (WS) Sl 1 pwise wyf, knit to the last st, p1.

Row 2: (RS) Sl 1 kwise, **k2tog tbl,** k14, sl 1 kwise, k2tog, psso, k14, **k2tog,** p1—33 sts.

Row 3 and all WS rows: (WS) Sl 1 kwise, knit to the last st, p1.

Row 4: Sl 1 kwise, k2tog tbl, k12, sl 1 **kwise,** k2tog, psso, k12, k2tog, p1—29 sts.

Row 6: Sl 1 kwise, k2tog tbl, knit to center 3 sts (i.e., k10), sl 1 kwise, k2tog, psso, knit to last 3 sts (i.e., k10), k2tog, p1—25 sts.

Row 8: Sl 1 kwise, k2tog tbl, knit to center 3 sts (i.e., k8), sl 1 kwise, k2tog, psso, knit to last 3 sts (i.e., k8), k2tog, p1—21 sts.

Cont to dec 1 st each end of needle and 2 sts at the center every other row until 5 sts.

Next row: (WS) Sl 1 kwise, k3, p1.

Next row: (RS) Sl 1 kwise, **K3tog,** p1—3 sts.

Next row: Sl 1 kwise, k1, p1.

Next row: K3tog—1 st rem. BO end st.

‹ Triangles 50 and 51

Foll the placement indicated on the chart, work as for Triangle 49.

FLAP

‹ *Squares 46, 47, and 48*
Foll the placement indicated on the chart,
work as for Square 19.

FINISHING

Weave in loose ends. Felt in the washing
machine according to the guidelines on
page 137.

NEEDLE-FELTED DOTS

Place the felting mat inside the backpack
and work needle-felted "dots" in the colors
and positions specified on the chart as foll:
Wrap the yarn 5 times around your index
finger, gently transfer the circle of yarn onto
the backpack as specified on the chart, and
use a needle-felting tool to felt the circle to
the bag.

LINING

Using the felted backpack as a guide, cut
the ***lining*** fabric. Sew the lining into a shape
to match the backpack, then insert it inside
the backpack with WS facing together, and
sew it in place. Lining should be slightly
larger than backpack.

CONTRASTING BINDING

Cut coordinating fabric into 2" (5 cm) widths
and sew together to form a piece long
enough to bind the felted fabric along the
opening and flap. With sharp-point sewing
needle and matching thread, sew binding
in place.

BUTTON LOOP

With black and dpn, CO 2 sts. Work 2-st
I-cord until piece is about 6" (15 cm) long.
BO all sts. Fold loop in half and sew to tip
of flap, hiding the ends in the contrasting
binding on the WS of the flap.

TASSEL

With Red, make a ***tassel,*** wrapping the
yarn 40 times around a 4" (10 cm) piece of
cardboard. Sew tassel to bottom point of
backpack.

D-RING TABS (MAKE 2)

With Black, CO 16 sts. Work double knitting
as foll: *K1, sl 1 pwise with yarn in front
(wyf); rep from *. Rep this row until piece
measures about 2½" (6.5 cm) from CO. BO
all sts as foll: K1, *k2tog, pass the knitted
st over the decreased st; rep from *, ending
with k1, pass over, and BO the last st. Sew
a D-ring to the center of each tab, then sew
the tabs securely to the lower corners of the
backpack back.

STRAPS

Sew the center 6" to 7" (16 to 18 cm) of
webbing to center back of backpack, about
even with the front opening as shown at left.
Fold the end of each strap around a snap
hook and sew them securely in place. Hook
the snap hooks to the D-rings.

With sharp-point sewing needle and matching thread, sew the button to the front of the
backpack, opposite the buttonhole when
the flap is folded over the opening.

slippers

These comfy slippers are adapted from traditional Faroese-Icelandic shoes.
They begin with two blocks (consisting of one square each) joined along two
sides to form the closed toe. Additional squares are added to this pouch to
form the sides, sole, heel, and optional ankle. Depending on how you work the
final two squares or triangles at the ankle, you can leave the top edge as is,
or finish it off with a simple round of crochet, a knitted ribbing, or a folded edge
and decorative tie. Felt the slippers in the washing machine to shrink them to
size, then brush on a layer of latex on the soles to give them a nonslip sole.

[materials]

FINISHED SIZE Use the sizing table on page 54 to help you
determine slipper size. But keep in mind that felting is inexact
and it's not possible to predict a specific size. Even the same yarn
knitted to the same gauge will felt differently depending on the
color of the yarn, the water temperature, the amount of agitation,
and the type of soap. If your slippers end up smaller or larger than
expected, try again following the instructions for a larger or smaller
size. Give the extra slippers as gifts and get smiles in return.

YARN Fingering weight (#1 Super Fine) in 2 or more colors.
Shown here: New England Knitter's Shetland (100% wool; 217
yd [200 m]/50 g): 2 or more colors. General guideline for yarn
amounts: 1 to 1½ skeins for children's sizes 9½ to 11½; 1½ to 1¾
skeins for sizes 12 to 1½; 1¾ to 2 skeins for sizes 2½ to 5; 2 to 2¼
skeins for sizes 6 to 8; 2½ to 3¼ skeins for sizes 8½ to 11½.
The exact amount of each color depends on the number of colors,
style, and the finished size.

NEEDLES U.S. size 4 or 6 (3.5 or 4 mm): domino needles (page 6)
and double-pointed needles (dpn) for knitted cuff. Adjust needle size
if necessary to obtain the correct gauge.

NOTIONS Tapestry needle; latex or puff paint (available at
craft stores) for reinforcing soles and helping to prevent slipping
(optional); size B/1 (2.25 mm) crochet hook for picot crochet
edging (optional); sharp-point sewing needle and matching thread
for forming drawstring casing (optional); marker (m) for knitted
cuff; 4 small bells to attach to ends of drawstrings (optional).

GAUGE See sizing table on page 57.

[techniques]

▼ knit squares and blocks (page 9)

▼ reading charts (page 10)

▼ join two blocks into a pouch (page 30)

▼ weave in tails as you knit (page 12)

▼ see Glossary (page 133) for abbreviations and highlighted terms

[notes]

▸ Work the squares in garter stitch.
▸ The number of stitches in each square depends on the desired slipper size.

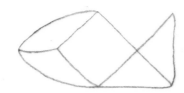

SLIPPER WITH 6 SQUARES

The slipper shown was worked on 39-stitch garter-stitch squares in Iris and Lilac for a finished U.S. children's shoe size of 9½.

SLIPPER SIZING

U.S. Shoe Size	Foot length	1 Square*
9½	6¾"/17 cm	5⅜"/13.5 cm
10½	6⅞"/17.5 cm	5½"/14 cm
11½	7⅛"/18 cm	5¾"/14.5 cm
12	7½"/19 cm	5⅞"/15 cm
13	7¾"/19.5 cm	6⅛"/15.5 cm
1	7⅞"/20 cm	6¼"/16 cm
1½	8¼"/21 cm	6½"/16.5 cm
2½	8½"/21.5 cm	6¾"/17 cm
3½	8¾"/22.5 cm	6⅞"/17.5 cm
4½	9"/23 cm	7⅛"/18 cm
5	9½"/24 cm	7¼"/18.5 cm
6	9⅝"/24.5 cm	7½"/19 cm
7	9⅞"/25 cm	7¾"/19.5 cm
7½	10¼"/26 cm	7⅞"/20 cm
8	10⅜"/26.5 cm	8⅛"/20.5 cm
8½	10⅝"/27 cm	8¼"/21 cm
9	11"/28 cm	8½"/21.5 cm
10½	11¼"/28.5 cm	8¾"/22 cm
11½	11⅜"/29 cm	8⅞"/22.5 cm

* measured diagonally, before felting

‹ Square 1 (top of toes)

With Iris, **K-CO** 25 (27, 29, 31, 33, 35, 37, 39, 41, 43, 45, 47, 49, 51, 53, 55, 57) sts.
Row 1: (WS) Knit to the last st, p1 (**edge st**).
Row 2: (RS) Sl 1 kwise (edge st), knit to 1 st before center st, **sl 1 kwise, k2tog, psso**, knit to last st, p1 (edge st)—2 sts decreased.
Row 3: Sl 1 kwise, knit to last st, p1.
Rep Rows 2 and 3, changing between Iris and Lilac every 6 rows (3 garter ridges on RS) until 3 sts rem on a RS row.
Next row: (WS) Sl 1 kwise, k1, p1.
Next row: (RS) Sl 1 kwise, k2tog, psso—1 st rem (**end st**). **BO** the end st.

‹ Square 2 (bottom of toes)

Rotate Square 1 so CO edge is at the top. With Lilac, RS of Square 1 facing, and working from right to left, **pick-knit** 25 (27, 29, 31, 33, 35, 37, 39, 41, 43, 45, 47, 49, 51, 53, 55, 57) sts (1 st in each CO loop and 1 st in top corner) along top of Square 1. Work as for Square 1 but beg the first row with sl 1 pwise with yarn in front (wyf) and work the colors in the opposite order.

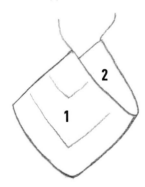

‹ Square 3 (one side of foot)

Rotate piece so end st of Squares 1 and 2 are at the top. With Iris and working from right to left, pick-knit 25 (27, 29, 31, 33, 35, 37, 39, 41, 43, 45, 47, 49, 51, 53, 55, 57) sts between the end sts Squares 2 and 1, pick-knitting the center st between the two squares. Work as for Square 1 but beg the first row with sl 1 pwise wyf.

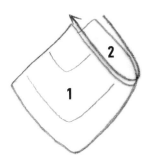

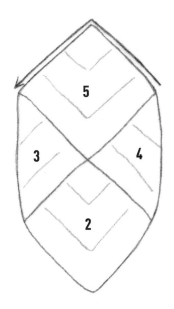

Square 4 (opposite side of foot)

With Iris and working from right to left on the other side of Squares 1 and 2, pick-knit 25 (27, 29, 31, 33, 35, 37, 39, 41, 43, 45, 47, 49, 51, 53, 55, 57) sts between the end sts of Squares 1 and 2, pick-knitting the center st between the two squares. Work as for Square 1 but beg the first row with sl 1 pwise wyf.

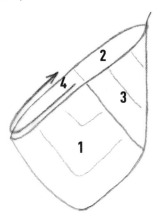

Square 5 (bottom of heel)

With Lilac, pick-knit 25 (27, 29, 31, 33, 35, 37, 39, 41, 43, 45, 47, 49, 51, 53, 55, 57) sts between the end sts of Squares 3 and 4, pick-knitting the center st in the tip of the square below. Work as for Square 1 but beg the first row with sl 1 pwise wyf and work the colors in the opposite order.

Square 6 (back of heel)

With the bottom of the slipper (RS of Square 5) facing, Iris and working from right to left, pick-knit 25 (27, 29, 31, 33, 35, 37, 39, 41, 43, 45, 47, 49, 51, 53, 55, 57) sts (1 st in each edge st) along the top of Square 5. Work as for Square 1 but beg the first row with sl 1 pwise wyf.

FINISHING

Weave in loose ends. Felt in the washing machine according to the guidelines on page 137. Trace the outline of each foot (while standing) on a piece of stiff plastic. While the felted slippers are still wet, insert the plastic into the slippers, stretching and shaping the fabric as necessary to accommodate the plastic. Allow to thoroughly air-dry before removing the plastic.

PICOT CROCHET EDGING

With Iris, crochet hook, RS facing and beg in the notch between Squares 3 and 6, work around slipper opening as foll: *Insert hook about ¼" (6 mm) down from top edge, yarn over hook and pull up a loop ¼" (6 mm) long, [insert hook ¼" (6 mm) from top edge and about 1 st to the left of last loop, yarn over and pull up a loop ¼" (6 mm) long] 2 times, yarn over hook and pull through all 3 loops on hook, ch 3, work 1 sl st in first ch to make a picot. Move to the left (about 2 sts) and rep from *. Rep from * to * around the entire top edge of slipper, end with sl st in the first st made between Square 3 and 6. If desired, make a loop for hanging the slipper by working a chain 15 sts long at the back of the heel (tip of Square 6) instead of a picot, then cont in patt to end of rnd.

LATEX OR PUFF PAINT

To give a nonskid finish to the soles and to make them wear longer, brush several coats of latex or squirt puff paint on the bottom of the slippers, letting each coat dry before applying the next one.

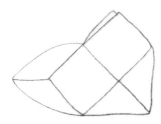 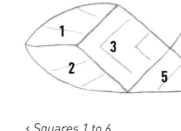 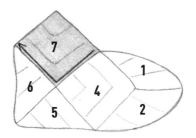

SLIPPER WITH 8 SQUARES

The slipper shown was worked on 47-stitch garter-stitch squares in stripes of Tundra, Midnight Blue, Seagreen, and Iris for a finished U.S. shoe size of 2½. The slippers shown weigh about 3 oz (82 g). They are worked as for the Slipper with 6 Squares, with additional squares added at the ankles.

‹ *Squares 1 to 6*

Working stripes as desired, work as for Squares 1 to 6 of Slipper with 6 Squares (page 54).

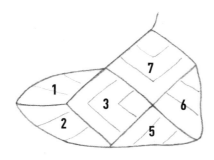

‹ *Square 7 (ankle side)*

With Seagreen, **pick-knit** 25 (27, 29, 31, 33, 35, 37, 39, 41, 43, 45, 47, 49, 51, 53, 55, 57) sts along Squares 6 and 3, pick-knitting the center st at the tip of Square 5. Work as for Square 1 but beg the first row with sl 1 pwise with yarn in front (wyf).

‹ *Square 8 (ankle side)*

Rotate the slipper so that Square 4 is facing. With Seagreen, pick-knit 25 (27, 29, 31, 33, 35, 37, 39, 41, 43, 45, 47, 49, 51, 53, 55, 57) sts along Squares 4 and 6, pick-knitting the center st at the tip of Square 5. Work as for Square 1 but beg the first row with sl 1 pwise wyf.

FINISHING

Weave in loose ends. Felt and shape and add latex as for Slipper with 6 Squares (pages 55 and 56).

CUFF

Fold Squares 7 and 8 to the inside of the slipper and with a double strand of sewing threaded on a sharp-point needle, use a **backstitch** to secure to WS of slipper, creating a casing for a drawstring.

DRAWSTRING

With Iris, CO 4 sts. Work 4-st **I-cord** until piece is long enough to thread inside the casing around ankle with ends long enough to tie into a bow. BO all sts. Beg and ending at the center front, pull drawstring through casing. Knot the ends of the drawstring. Tie drawstring in a bow.

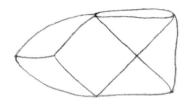

SLIPPER WITH 6 SQUARES AND 2 TRIANGLES

The slipper shown was worked on 37-stitch garter-stitch squares in stripes of Magenta and Gold for a finished U.S. shoe size of 1. The pair of slippers shown weighs about 1½ oz (42 g). It is worked as for the Slipper with 6 Squares, with a triangle added at each side of the ankle.

‹ *Squares 1 to 6*

Substituting Gold for Iris and Magenta for Lady Slipper, work as for Squares 1 to 6 of Slipper with 6 Squares (page 56).

‹ *Triangle 1 (ankle side)*

With Magenta, pick-knit 25 (27, 29, 31, 33, 35, 37, 39, 41, 43, 45, 47, 49, 51, 53, 55, 57) sts along Squares 6 and 3, pick-knitting the center st at the tip of Square 5.

Row 1: (WS) Sl 1 wyf, knit to the last st, p1 (edge st).

Row 2: (RS) Sl 1, *k2tog tbl,* knit to 1 st before center st, sl 1 kwise, k2tog, psso, knit to last 3 sts, *k2tog,* p1—4 sts decreased.

Row 3 and all WS rows: Sl 1 kwise, knit to last st, p1.

Rep Rows 2 and 3, dec 1 st each end of needle and 2 sts at the center of needle every other row until either 5 or 7 sts. If 5 sts rem, cont as foll:

Next row: (WS) Sl 1 kwise, k3, p1.

Next row: Sl 1 kwise, sl 1 kwise, k2tog, psso, p1—3 sts.

Next row: Sl 1 kwise, k1, p1.

Next row: (RS): *K3tog*—1 st rem. *BO* end st. If 7 sts rem, cont as foll:

Next row: (WS) K2tog tbl, [k2tog] 2 times, pass the second and third st over the first, then BO the end st.

‹ *Triangle 2 (ankle side)*

With Magenta, pick-knit 25 (27, 29, 31, 33, 35, 37, 39, 41, 43, 45, 47, 49, 51, 53, 55, 57) sts along Squares 4 and 6, pick-knitting the center st at the tip of Square 5. Work as for Triangle 1.

FINISHING

Weave in loose ends. Felt and shape and add latex as for Slipper with 6 Squares (pages 55 and 56).

CUFF

With Magenta and double-pointed needles, K-CO the appropriate number of sts to fit comfortably around wearer's ankle. Place marker (pm) and join for working in rnds, being careful not to twist sts. Work in k1, p1 rib until piece measures 2" (5 cm) from CO. BO all sts loosely. With Magenta threaded on a tapestry needle, sew RS of cuff to RS of slipper opening.

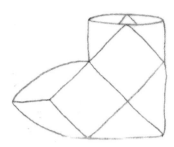

SLIPPER WITH 8 SQUARES AND 2 TRIANGLES

The slipper shown was worked on 35-stitch garter-stitch squares in stripes of Lady Slipper and Poppy for a finished U.S. children's shoe size of 9½. The pair of slippers weighs 1¾ oz (49 grams). They are worked as for Slipper with 8 Squares, with additional triangles added at the ankles.

‹ *Squares 1 to 6*
Substituting Lady Slipper for Iris and Poppy for Lady Slipper, work as for Squares 1 to 6 of Slipper with 6 Squares (page 54).

‹ *Square 7 (ankle side)*
With Lady Slipper, **pick-knit** 25 (27, 29, 31, 33, 35, 37, 39, 41, 43, 45, 47, 49, 51, 53, 55, 57) sts along Squares 6 and 3, pick-knitting the center st at the tip of Square 5. Work as for Square 1 but beg the first row with sl 1 pwise with yarn in front (wyf).

‹ *Square 8 (ankle side)*
Rotate the slipper so that Square 4 is facing. With Lady Slipper, pick-knit 25 (27, 29, 31, 33, 35, 37, 39, 41, 43, 45, 47, 49, 51, 53, 55, 57) sts along Squares 4 and 6, pick-knitting the center st at the tip of Square 5. Work as for Square 1 but beg the first row with sl 1 wyf.

‹ *Triangle 1 (ankle back)*
With Poppy, pick-knit 25 (27, 29, 31, 33, 35, 37, 39, 41, 43, 45, 47, 49, 51, 53, 55, 57) sts along the top of Squares 8 and 7, pick-knitting the center st at the tip of Square 6.
Row 1: (WS) Sl 1 pwise wyf, knit to the last st, p1 (edge st).
Row 2: (RS) Sl 1, **k2tog tbl**, knit to 1 st before center st, **sl 1 kwise, k2tog, psso,** knit to last 3 sts, **k2tog,** p1—4 sts decreased.
Row 3 and all WS rows: Sl 1 kwise, knit to last st, p1.
Rep Rows 2 and 3, dec 1 st each end of needle and 2 sts at the center of needle every other row until either 5 or 7 sts.
If 5 sts rem, cont as foll:
Next row: (WS) Sl 1, k3, p1.
Next row: Sl 1 kwise, sl 1 kwise, k2tog, psso, p1—3 sts.
Next row: Sl 1 kwise, k1, p1.

Next row: (RS): K3tog—1 st rem. **BO** end st.
If 7 sts rem, cont as foll:
Next row: (WS) K2tog tbl, [k2tog] 2 times, pass the second and third st over the first, then BO the end st.

‹ *Triangle 2 (ankle front)*
With Poppy, pick-knit 25 (27, 29, 31, 33, 35, 37, 39, 41, 43, 45, 47, 49, 51, 53, 55, 57) sts along to top of Squares 7 and 8, pick-knitting the center st at the tip of Square 3. Work as for Triangle 1.

FINISHING

Weave in loose ends. Felt and shape and add latex as for Slipper with 6 Squares (pages 55 and 56).

DECORATIVE TIES (make 2)

With Poppy and double-pointed needles, CO 2 sts. Work 2-st **I-cord** until piece measures about 8" to 10" (20.5 to 25.5 cm). BO all sts. With Poppy threaded on a tapestry needle, sew one bell to each end of tie, if desired. Sew center of tie to center front of slipper and tie into a bow.

chapter three
join three blocks into a pouch

Join three blocks (or squares) to form a large pouch or pocket that can be the basis for a hat or tea or coffee cozy. The sample blocks shown here consist of nine squares (three panels of three squares each). Each square begins with 25 stitches and is worked in garter stitch. Different colors are used here so the individual squares are easy to see.

BLOCK 1

Knit and join Square 1 to 9 as described on page 8, working each square in a solid color.

BLOCK 2

This block is worked along one side of Block 1, as described on page 20. Rotate Block 1 counterclockwise so that Squares 9, 8, and 7 (Panel 3) are at the top.

Rep Rows 4 and 5 until 3 sts rem on a RS row.

Next row: (WS) Sl 1 kwise, k1, p1.

Next row: Sl 1 kwise, k2tog, psso—1 st rem (***end st***). Leave this st on the needle.

‹ *Square 11*

This square will fill the notch between Squares 10, 1, and 4. Using the end st from Square 10 as the first st of Square 11, pick-knit 11 sts along the upper edge of Square 10 (12 sts on needle), 1 st in the tip of Square 1, and 12 sts along the right edge of Square 4 (1 st in each CO loop)—25 sts total.

Work as for Square 10—1 st rem (end st).

PANEL 1

‹ *Square 10*

K-CO 13 sts, place the needle in your right hand, and ***pick-knit*** 12 sts along the right edge of Square 1 (1 st in each CO loop)—25 sts total.

Row 1: (WS) Sl 1 pwise with yarn in front (wyf), knit to the last st, p1 (***edge st***).

Row 2: (RS) Sl 1 kwise (edge st), k10, ***sl 1 kwise, k2tog, psso,*** k10, p1 (edge st)—23 sts.

Row 3: Sl 1 kwise, knit to the last st, p1.

Row 4: Sl 1 kwise, knit to 1 st before the center st (i.e., k9), sl 1 kwise, k2tog, psso, knit to the last st (i.e., k9), p1—21 sts.

Row 5: Sl 1 kwise, knit to the last st, p1.

‹ *Square 12*

Using the end st from Square 11 as the first st of Square 12, pick-knit 11 sts along the upper edge of Square 11 (12 sts on needle), 1 st in the tip of Square 4, and 12 sts along the right edge of Square 7—25 sts total. Work as for Square 10 but end by pulling the end st loose, cutting the yarn, and threading the tail through it.

PANEL 2

‹ Square 13

K-CO 12 sts, place the needle in your right hand, pick-knit 1 st **"around the corner"** *under* the lower right corner of Square 10, and 12 sts along the right edge of Square 10 (1 st in each edge st)—25 sts total. Work as for Square 10 but beg the first row with sl 1 pwise with yarn in front (wyf).

‹ Square 14

Using the end st from Square 13 as the first st of Square 14, pick-knit 11 sts along the upper edge of Square 13 (12 sts on needle), 1 st in the tip of Square 10, and 12 sts along the right edge of Square 11—25 sts total. Work as for Square 10.

‹ Square 15

Using the end st from Square 14 as the first st of Square 15, pick-knit 11 sts along the upper edge of Square 14 (12 sts on needle), 1 st in the tip of Square 11, 11 sts along the right edge of Square 12, and 1 st in the end st of Square 12—25 sts total. Work as for Square 10 but end by pulling the end st loose, cutting the yarn, and threading the tail through it.

BLOCK 3
PANEL 1
‹ Square 19

This square will form a pyramid with Squares 1 and 10. Rotate the piece so that Squares 16, 13, 10, 1, 2, and 3 are at the top. With RS facing and working from right to left, pick-knit 25 sts along Squares 1 and 10, (1 st in each CO loop), pick-knitting the center st in boundary between Square 1 and Square 10—25 sts total. Work as for Square 10.

PANEL 3
‹ Squares 16, 17, and 18

Work as for Squares 13, 14, and 15, pick-knitting sts along right edge of Squares 13, 14, and 15. BO the end st of Square 18.

‹ Square 20

Using the end st of Square 19 as the first st of Square 20, pick-knit 11 sts along the left edge of Square 19 (12 sts on needle), 1 st in the tip of Square 10, and 12 sts along the edge of Square 13—25 sts total. Work as for Square 10.

‹ Square 21

Using the end st of Square 20 as the first st of Square 21, pick-knit 11 sts along the upper edge of Square 20 (12 sts on needle), 1 st in the tip of Square 13, and 12 sts along the right edge of Square 16—25 sts total. Work as for Square 10 but end by pulling the end st loose, cutting the yarn, and threading the tail through it.

PANEL 2
‹ Square 22

Working from right to left, pick-knit 25 st along Squares 2 and 19, pick-knitting the center st in the tip of Square 1. Work as for Square 10.

‹ Square 23

Using the end st from Square 22 as the first st of Square 23, pick-knit 11 sts along the upper edge of Square 22 (12 sts on needle), 1 st in the tip of Square 19, and 12 sts along the right edge of Square 20—25 sts total. Work as for Square 10.

‹ Square 24

Using the end st of Square 23 as the first st of Square 24, pick-knit 11 sts along the upper edge of Square 22 (12 sts on needle), 1 st in the tip of Square 20, 11 sts along the right edge of Square 21, and 1 st in the end st of Square 21—25 sts total. Work as for Square 10 but end by pulling the end st loose, cutting the yarn, and threading the tail through it.

PANEL 3
‹ Square 25

Working from right to left, pick-knit 25 st along Squares 3 and 22, pick-knitting the center st in the tip of Square 2. Work as for Square 10.

‹ Square 26

Using the end st from Square 25 as the first st of Square 26, pick-knit 11 sts along the upper edge of Square 25 (12 sts on needle), 1 st in the tip of Square 22, and 12 sts along the right edge of Square 23—25 sts total. Work as for Square 10.

‹ Square 27

Using the end st of Square 26 as the first st of Square 27, pick-knit 11 sts along the top of Square 26 (12 sts on needle), 1 st in the end st of Square 23, and 12 sts along the right edge of Square 24—25 sts total. Work as for Square 10 but end by pulling end st loose, cutting the yarn, and threading the tail through it. BO the end st.

three-block cap

This jester-style cap is made up of three nine-square blocks (consisting of three panels of three squares each) that are joined together into a point to form the crown. The notches between the blocks are filled in with additional squares and end with triangles to give a straight edge at the "brim." By adjusting the number of stitches worked in each square, you can size the hat for a small, medium, or large head. Finish the lower edge with ribbing for a tighter fit or with a simple rolled edge for a looser fit. Experiment with different color combinations in the squares for completely different looks.

[materials]

FINISHED SIZE About 19¼ (21¼, 23¼)" (49 [54, 59] cm) in diameter. To fit child (adult small) adult large. Hat shown measures 23¼" (59 cm). **Note:** The exact size depends on the type of yarn and the size of the squares. If the cap is too loose, work a tight edging.

YARN Fingering weight (#1 Super Fine) in 5 colors.

Shown here: Harrisville New England Knitter's Shetland (100% wool; 217 yd [200 m]/50 g): Foliage, Garnet, Blackberry, Magenta, and Red, less than 1 skein each.

NEEDLES Size 3 mm (between U.S. size 2 and 3): domino needles (page 6). Size 2.5 mm (between U.S. size 1 and 2): 16" (40 cm) circular (cir). Adjust needle size if necessary to obtain the correct gauge.

NOTIONS Tapestry needle.

GAUGE 1 square measures 1.6 by 1.6 (1.8 by 1.8, 2 by 2)" (4 by 4 [4.7 by 4.7, 5 by 5] cm) and 2.4 (2.4, 2.5)" (6 [6, 6.5] cm) on the diagonal.

[techniques]

▸ knit squares and blocks (page 9)
▸ reading charts (page 10)
▸ join three blocks into a pouch (page 60)
▸ weave in tails as you knit (page 12)
▸ see Glossary (page 133) for abbreviations and highlighted terms

[notes]

▼ To make a three-dimensional model of the cap, make a photocopy of the chart, cut it out, and tape it together connecting Squares 34 and 36 and Triangle 45 to Squares 3, 6, and 9, and connecting Squares 1, 10, and 19 together at a point.

▼ Work the squares and triangles in numerical order in the colors specified (indicated by letters) on the chart. The direction of the numbers on the chart indicates the knitting direction.

▼ Each square is worked in garter stitch in two colors that alternate color every two rows. See the chart for the color combinations.

BLOCK 1
PANEL 1
‹ Square 1

With Red, **K-CO** 21 (23, 25) sts. Work in garter-stitch stripes, changing colors every other row and twisting yarns at color changes for a **twisted selvedge** as foll.

Row 1: (WS) Knit to the last st, p1 (**edge st**).

Row 2: (RS) Change to Foliage. Sl 1 kwise (edge st), knit to 1 st before center st (i.e., k9 [10, 11]), **sl 1 kwise, k2tog, psso,** knit to last st, p1 (edge st)—2 sts decreased.

Row 3: Sl 1 kwise (edge st), knit to last st, p1 (edge st).

Rep Rows 2 and 3, changing between Foliage and Red every other row until 3 sts rem on a RS row.

Next row: (WS) Sl 1 kwise, k1, p1.

Next row: (RS) Sl 1 kwise, k2tog, psso—1 st rem (**end st**).

‹ Square 2

Using the end st from Square 1 as the first st of Square 2, with Blackberry, **pick-knit** 9 (10, 11) sts along the upper edge of Square 1 (**Note:** Skip the first edge st because the end st from Square 1 is now the first st of Square 2; it doesn't matter that it's a different color), go **"around the corner"** and pick-knit 1 st in the nearest CO loop, **turn work**, and K-CO 10 (11, 12) new sts—21 (23, 25) sts total. Work as for Square 1, cont changing between Blackberry and Magenta.

‹ Square 3

With the colors specified on the chart, work as for Square 2, pick-knitting sts at the top of Square 2 and ending by pulling the end st loose, cutting the yarn, and threading the tail through it.

PANEL 2
‹ Square 4

With Foliage, K-CO 10 (11, 12) sts, place the needle in your right hand and pick-knit 1 st "around the corner" *under* Square 1 in the far right CO loop, then pick-knit 10 (11, 12) sts along the right edge of Square 1—21 (23, 25) sts total. Work as for Square 1, but beg the first row with sl 1 pwise with yarn in front (wyf), cont alternating between Foliage and Garnet.

‹ Square 5

Foll the placement and colors indicated on the chart, work as for Square 2, always beginning at the top of the square just completed and the side of the corresponding square of the previous panel.

‹ Square 6

Work as for Square 5, but when pick-knitting sts, pick-knit the last st in the end st of Square 3 (pull the tail tight to secure the st). End by pulling the end st loose, cutting the yarn, and threading the tail through it.

PANEL 3

Foll the placement and colors indicated on the chart, work Squares 7, 8, and 9 as for Squares 4, 5, and 6 of Panel 2. **BO** the end st of Square 9.

BLOCK 2
PANEL 1

Rotate Block 1 so that Panel 3 (Squares 7, 8, and 9) is at the top. Work Block 2 to the right of Block 1, connecting it to Squares 1, 4, and 7 as follows.

‹ Square 10

With Magenta, K-CO 11 (12, 13) sts, place the needle in your right hand and pick-knit 10 (11, 12) sts (1 st in each CO loop) along the upper edge of Square 1 (working

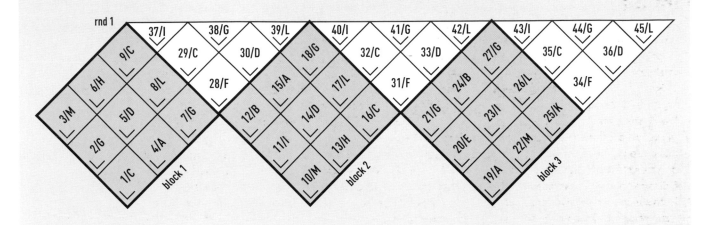

rnd 1

| block 1 | | | | block 2 | | | | block 3 | | |

Diagram labels:
- rnd 1
- 37/I 38/G 39/L 40/I 41/G 42/L 43/I 44/G 45/L
- 9/C 29/C 30/D 18/G 32/C 33/D 27/G 35/C 36/D
- 6/H 8/L 28/F 15/A 17/L 31/F 24/B 26/L 34/F
- 3/M 5/D 7/G 12/B 14/D 16/C 21/G 23/I 25/K
- 2/G 4/A 11/I 13/H 20/E 22/M
- 1/C 10/M 19/A
- block 1 block 2 block 3

COLOR KEY

K-CO or pick-knit with the first color, then knit 1 row with the same color, then alternate 2 rows each of the two colors, twisting the yarns around each other at color changes.

A: Foliage and Garnet
B: Foliage and Red
C: Red and Foliage
D: Magenta and Foliage
E: Foliage and Magenta
F: Garnet and Foliage
G: Blackberry and Magenta
H: Magenta and Blackberry
I: Blackberry and Red
K: Red and Blackberry
L: Garnet and Magenta
M: Magenta and Garnet

toward Square 4)—21 (23, 25) sts total. Work as for Square 1 but beg the first row with sl 1 pwise wyf, cont alternating between Magenta and Garnet.

‹ Square 11

Using the end st from Square 10 as the first st of Square 11, pick-knit 10 (11, 12) sts along left edge of Square 10, 1 st between Squares 1 and 4, and 10 (11, 12) sts along the right edge of Square 4—21 (23, 25) sts total. Work as for Square 1 but beg the first row with sl 1 pwise wyf, cont alternating between Blackberry and Red.

‹ Square 12

With the colors specified on the chart, work as for Square 11, pick-knitting sts along the upper edge of Square 11, 1 st between Squares 7 and 4, and along the right edge of Square 7. End by pulling the end st loose, cutting the yarn, and threading the tail through it.

PANEL 2

Foll the placement and colors specified on the chart, work Squares 13, 14, and 15 as for Squares 4, 5, and 6 (Panel 2) of Block 1.

PANEL 3

Foll the placement and colors specified on the chart, work Squares 16, 17, and 18 as for Squares 7, 8, and 9 (Panel 3) of Block 1. BO the end st of Square 18.

BLOCK 3

Rotate the piece so that Squares 16, 13, 10, 1, 2, and 3 are at the top.

PANEL 1

‹ Square 19

With Foliage, pick-knit 21 (23, 25) sts in the CO loops of Squares 1 and 10, pick-knit-

ting the center st between Squares 1 and 10. Work as for Square 1 but beg the first row with sl 1 pwise wyf, cont alternating between Foliage and Garnet.

‹ Squares 20 and 21

Foll the placement and colors specified on the chart, work as for Squares 11 and 12 of Block 2.

PANELS 2 AND 3

Foll the placement and colors specified on the chart, work Squares 22 to 27 as for Squares 13 to 18 (Panels 2 and 3) of Block 2. BO the end st of Square 27. The piece will now have the shape of a three-sided bowl.

FILL IN GAPS BETWEEN BLOCKS

‹ Square 28

With Garnet, pick-knit 21 (23, 25) sts along the edge of Squares 12 and 7, pick-knitting the center st between Squares 12 and 7. Work as for Square 1 but beg the first row with sl 1 pwise wyf, cont alternating between Garnet and Foliage.

‹ Square 29

Using the end st of Square 28 as the first st of Square 29, with Red, pick-knit 10 (11, 12) sts along the upper edge of Square 28, 1 st in the tip of Square 7, and 10 (11, 12) sts along the right edge of Square 8—21 (23) 25 sts total. Work as for Square 1 but beg the first row with sl 1 pwise wyf, cont alternating between Red and Foliage. BO the end st.

‹ Square 30

With Magenta, pick-knit 10 (11, 12) sts along the edge of Square 15, 1 st at the tip of Square 12, and 10 (11, 12) sts along the side of Square 28. Work as for Square 1 but

beg the first row with sl 1 pwise wyf, cont alternating between Magenta and Foliage. BO the end st.

‹ Squares 31, 32, and 33

Foll the placement and colors specified on the chart and working in the notch between Block 2 and Block 3, work as for Squares 28 to 30.

‹ Squares 34, 35, and 36

Foll the placement and colors specified on the chart and working in the notch between Block 3 and Block 1, work as for Squares 28 to 30.

ROUND 1

Work a triangle in each notch between Squares 9, 29, 30, 18, 32, 33, 27, 35, and 36 as foll.

‹ Triangle 37

With Blackberry, pick-knit 10 (11, 12) sts along the left edge of Square 29, 1 st in the tip of Square 8, and 10 (11, 12) sts along the right edge of Square 9—21 (23, 25) sts total.

Row 1: (WS) Sl 1 pwise wyf, knit to the last st, p1.

Row 2: (RS) Change to Red. Sl 1 kwise, *k2tog tbl,* knit to 1 st before center st, sl 1 kwise, k2tog, psso, knit to last 3 sts, *k2tog,* p1—4 sts decreased.

Row 3 and all foll WS rows: Sl 1 kwise, knit to last st, p1.

Rep Rows 2 and 3, dec 1 st each end of needle and 2 sts at the center of needle every other row and alternating between Red and Blackberry every 2 rows until either 5 or 7 sts rem.

If 5 sts rem, cont as foll:

Next row: (WS) Sl 1 kwise, k3, p1.

Next row: Sl 1 kwise (edge st), sl 1 kwise, k2tog, psso, p1—3 sts.

Next row: Sl 1 kwise, k1, p1.

Next row: (RS) *K3tog*—1 st rem. BO end st. If 7 sts rem, cont as foll:

Next row: K2tog tbl, [k2tog] 2 times, pass the second and third st over the first, then BO the rem st.

‹ *Triangles 38 to 45*

Foll the placement and colors specified on the chart, work as for Triangle 37.

FINISHING

Weave in loose ends.

ROLLED EDGE

With Garnet, cir needle, and RS facing, pick-knit 11 (12, 13) sts along each triangle—99 (108, 117) sts total. Join for working in rnds. Knit 17 rnds. Loosely BO all sts, allowing edging to roll to RS.

dotted tea cozy

This striking tea cozy follows the same principle as the three-block cap on page 64 (three blocks consisting of nine squares each), but more squares are worked around the circumference of the initial three-block pouch to add overall length. Triangles fill in the gaps between the final row of squares. The last few rows of each block are worked in a bright color to add lively dots to the purple base. The base is finished off with a simple rolled edge and the interior is lined with cotton fabric for added insulation. If a tea cozy isn't for you, turn the piece upside down, add a handle, replace the top loop with a tassel, and voilà—you've got a little purse instead!

[materials]

FINISHED SIZE About 32¾" (83 cm) around and 13¾" (35 cm) tall, before felting. About 26" (66 cm) around and 11½" (29 cm) tall, after felting.

YARN Fingering weight (#1 Super Fine) in 1 main color and 9 accent colors.

Shown here: Harrisville New England Knitter's Shetland (100% wool; 217 yd [200 m]/50 g): Aubergine (MC), 3 skeins; Tundra (A), Poppy (B), Lady Slipper (C), Periwinkle (D), Cornflower (E), Bermuda Blue (G), Gold (H), Magenta (I), and Seagreen (K), small amounts each.

NEEDLES Size 3 mm (between U.S. 2 and 3): domino needles (page 6) and 24" (60 cm) circular (cir). Adjust needle size if necessary to obtain the correct gauge.

NOTIONS Tapestry needle; about ½ yd (45.5 cm) cotton fabric for lining.

GAUGE Before felting: 1 square measures 2.4" by 2.4" (6.2 by 6.2 cm) and 3.6" (9.2 cm) on the diagonal. After felting: 1 square measures 2" by 2" (5.2 by 5.2 cm) and 2.9" (7.3 cm) on the diagonal.

[techniques]

◤ knit squares and blocks (page 9)
◤ reading charts (page 10)
◤ join three blocks into a pouch (page 60)
◤ weave in tails as you knit (page 12)
◤ see Glossary (page 133) for abbreviations and highlighted terms

[notes]

▼ To make a three-dimensional model of the tea cozy, make a photocopy of the chart, cut it out, and tape it together connecting Squares 34 and 45 and Triangle 63 to Squares 3, 36, and 46, and connecting Squares 1, 10, and 19 together at a point.

▼ Work the squares and triangles in numerical order in the colors specified on the chart. The direction of the numbers on the chart indicates the knitting direction.

▼ Each square is worked in garter stitch beginning with Aubergine and changing to a contrasting color after nineteen rows (ten garter ridges on the RS). See the chart for the color combinations.

BLOCK 1

PANEL 1

‹ *Square 1*

With MC, **K-CO** 29 sts. Work in garter-stitch stripes as foll:

Row 1: (WS) Knit to the last st, p1 *(edge st)*.

Row 2: (RS) Sl 1 kwise (edge st), knit to 1 st before center st (i.e., k12), *sl 1 kwise, k2tog, psso,* knit to last st (i.e., k12), p1 (edge st)—27 sts.

Row 3: Sl 1 kwise, knit to last st, p1.

Rep Rows 2 and 3, changing to Gold on Row 20 (10 garter ridges on RS), until 3 sts rem on a RS row.

Next row: (WS) Sl 1 kwise, k1, p1.

Next row: (RS) Sl 1 kwise, k2tog, psso—1 st rem *(end st)*.

‹ *Square 2*

Knit the end st from Square 1 with MC, then *pick-knit* 13 sts along the upper edge of Square 1, go *"around the corner"* and pick-knit 1 st in the nearest CO loop, *turn work,* and K-CO 14 new sts—29 sts total. Work as for Square 1, changing to Cornflower on Row 20.

‹ *Square 3*

With the colors specified on the chart, work as for Square 2, pick-knitting sts at the top of Square 2. End by pulling the end st loose, cutting the yarn, and threading the tail through it.

PANEL 2

‹ *Square 4*

With MC, K-CO 14 sts, pick-knit 1 st "around the corner" *under* Square 1 in the far right CO loop, then pick-knit 14 sts along the right edge of Square 1—29 sts total. Work as for Square 1 but beg the first row with sl 1 pwise with yarn in front (wyf) and change to Seagreen on Row 20.

‹ *Square 5*

Foll the placement and colors indicated on the chart, work as for Square 4, pick-knitting across the top of the square just completed and the side of the corresponding square of the previous panel.

‹ *Square 6*

Work as for Square 5, but when pick-knitting, pick-knit the last st in the end st of Square 3. End by pulling the end st loose, cutting the yarn, and threading the tail through it.

PANEL 3

Foll the placement and colors indicated on the chart, work Squares 7, 8, and 9 as for Squares 4, 5, and 6 of Panel 2. *BO* the end st of Square 9.

BLOCK 2

PANEL 1

Rotate Block 1 so that Panel 3 (Squares 9, 8, and 7) is at the top. Work Block 2 to the right of Block 1, connecting it to Squares 1, 4, and 7 as follows.

‹ *Square 10*

With MC, K-CO 15 sts, place the needle in your right hand, then pick-knit 14 sts (1 st in each CO loop) along the right edge of Square 1 (working toward Square 4)—29 sts total. Work as for Square 1 but beg the first row with sl 1 pwise wyf and change to Tundra on Row 20.

‹ *Square 11*

Knit the end st from Square 10 with MC and pick-knit 13 sts along the upper edge of Square 10, 1 st between Squares 1 and 4, and 14 sts along the right edge of Square 4—29 sts total. Work as for Square 1 but beg the first row with sl 1 pwise wyf and change to Lady Slipper on Row 20.

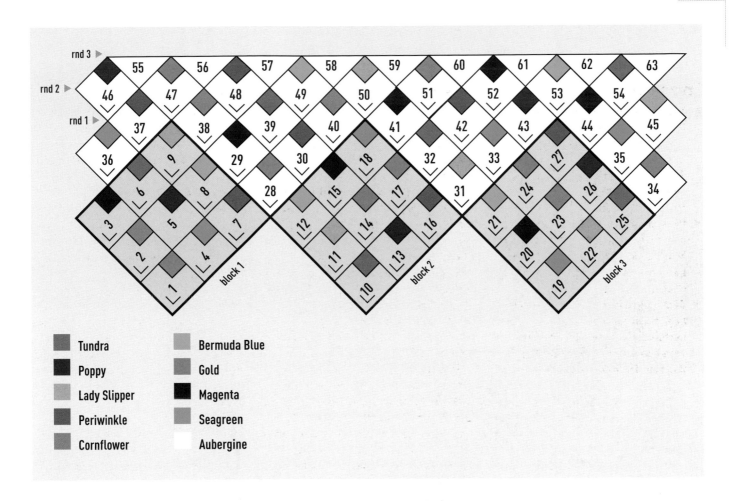

Tundra **Bermuda Blue**

Poppy **Gold**

Lady Slipper **Magenta**

Periwinkle **Seagreen**

Cornflower **Aubergine**

‹ *Square 12*

With the colors specified on the chart, work as for Square 11, pick-knitting sts along the upper edge of Square 11, 1 st between Squares 4 and 7, and along the upper edge of Square 7. End by pulling the end st loose, cutting the yarn, and threading the tail through it.

PANEL 2

Foll the placement and colors specified on the chart, work Squares 13, 14, and 15 as for Squares 4, 5, and 6 (Panel 2) of Block 1. When pick-knitting sts for Square 15, pick-knit the last st through the end st of

Square 12 (pull the tail to secure this st). End by pulling the end st loose, cutting the yarn, and threading the tail through it.

PANEL 3

Foll the placement and colors specified on the chart, work Squares 16, 17, and 18 as for Squares 7, 8, and 9 (Panel 3) of Block 1. BO the end st of Square 18.

BLOCK 3

Rotate the piece so that Squares 16, 13, 10, 1, 2, and 3 are at the top.

PANEL 1

‹ *Square 19*

With MC, pick-knit 29 sts along the edges of Squares 1 and 10, pick-knitting the center st in the boundary between Squares 1 and 10. Work as for Square 1 but beg the first row with sl 1 pwise wyf and change to Seagreen on Row 20.

‹ *Squares 20 and 21*

Foll the placement and colors specified on the chart, work as for Squares 11 and 12 of Block 2.

PANELS 2 AND 3

Foll the placement and colors specified on the chart, work Squares 22 to 27 as for Squares 13 to 18 (Panels 2 and 3) of Block 2. The piece will have the shape of a three-sided bowl.

FILL IN GAPS BETWEEN BLOCKS

‹ *Square 28*

With MC, pick-knit 29 sts along the edge of Squares 12 and 7, pick-knitting the center st between Squares 12 and 7. Work as for Square 1 but beg the first row with sl 1 pwise wyf and change to Gold on Row 20.

‹ *Square 29*

Knit the end st of Square 28 with MC, then pick-knit 13 sts along left edge of Square 28, 1 st in the tip of Square 7, and 14 sts along the right edge of Square 8—29 sts total. Work as for Square 1 but beg the first row with sl 1 pwise wyf and change to Magenta on Row 20. BO the end st.

‹ *Square 30*

With MC, pick-knit 14 sts along top edge of Square 15, 1 st at the tip of Square 12, and 14 sts along the side of Square 28—29 sts total. Work as for Square 1 but beg the first row with sl 1 pwise wyf and change to Periwinkle on Row 20. BO the end st.

‹ *Squares 31, 32, and 33*

Foll the placement and colors specified on the chart and working in the gap between Block 2 and Block 3, work as for Squares 28 to 30.

‹ *Squares 34, 35, and 36*

Foll the placement and colors specified on the chart and working in the gap between Block 3 and Block 1, work as for Squares 28 to 30.

ADD LENGTH IN ROUNDS

ROUND 1

‹ *Square 37*

With MC, pick-knit 14 sts along left edge of Square 9, 1 st in tip of Square 6, and 14 sts along right edge of Square 36—29 sts total. Work as for Square 1 but beg the first row with sl 1 pwise wyf and change to Seagreen on Row 20. BO the end st.

‹ *Squares 38 to 45*

Foll the placement and colors specified on the chart, work as for Square 37 but BO the end st of Square 45.

ROUND 2

Foll the placement and colors specified on the chart, work Squares 46 to 54 as for Squares 37 to 45 of Round 1.

ROUND 3

Work a triangle in each notch between the squares in Round 2 as follows.

‹ *Triangle 55*

With MC, pick-knit 14 sts along the left edge of Square 47, 1 st in the tip of Square 37, and 14 sts along the right edge of Square 46—29 sts total.

Row 1: (WS) Sl 1 pwise wyf, knit to the last st, p1.

Row 2: (RS) Sl 1, **k2tog tbl,** knit to 1 st before center st, sl 1 kwise, k2tog, psso, knit to last 3 sts, **k2tog,** p1—4 sts decreased.

Row 3: Sl 1 kwise, knit to last st, p1.

Rep Rows 2 and 3, dec 1 st each end of needle and 2 sts at the center of needle every other row until 5 sts rem.

Next row: (WS) Sl 1, k3, p1.

Next row: Sl 1 kwise (edge st), sl 1 kwise, k2tog, psso, p1—3 sts.

Next row: Sl 1 kwise, k1, p1.

Next row: (RS): **K3tog**—1 st rem. BO last st.

‹ *Triangles 56 to 63*

Foll the placement specified on the chart, work as for Triangle 55.

FINISHING

Weave in loose ends.

ROLLED EDGING

With MC and cir needle, pick-knit 15 sts along the edge of each triangle—135 sts total. Place marker (pm) and join for working in rnds. Purl 7 rnds. Loosely BO all sts, allowing edging to roll to WS.

FELTING

Felt the piece in the washing machine according to the guidelines on page 137.

TOP LOOP

With Magenta and dpn, K-CO 5 sts.

Row 1: [K1, yo in same st] 3 times, k1, sl 1 pwise with yarn in front (wyf)—8 sts.

Row 2: K1, [sl 1 pwise wyf, k1tbl] 3 times, sl 1 pwise wyf.

Row 3: [K1, sl 1 pwise wyf] 4 times.

Rep Row 3 until piece measures about 3¼" (8.5 cm) from CO.

Next row: K1, [k2tog, pass the second st over the first] 3 times, k1, pass the second st over the first—1 st rem. BO last st. Fold loop in half. With threaded tapestry needle, **whipstitch** both ends to top of cozy.

LINING

Add **lining** according to the instructions on page 138, if desired.

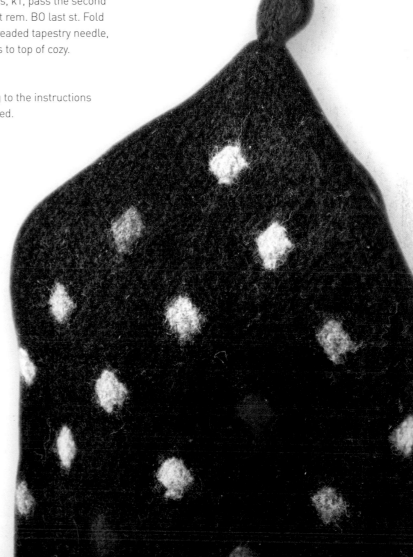

cape with fringe

The innovative shaping for the shoulders of this airy cape is based on three blocks (in this case, each block consists of a single square) joined together to form "points," just as for the crown of the Three-block Cap on page 64. Unlike other projects in this book, this cape isn't based on multiple blocks composed of multiple squares. Instead, the squares are added to one another in a somewhat random fashion to produce the unusual shape; be sure to follow the chart carefully to work the squares in the proper order. The squares that form the lower edges are punctuated with fringe that's formed by casting on then immediately binding off extra stitches.

[materials]

FINISHED SIZE About 28¼" (72 cm) across the back and 17" (43 cm) long from shoulder line to fringe.

YARN Sportweight (#2 Fine) in 4 colors.

Shown here: Rowan Kidsilk Haze (70% kid mohair, 30% silk; 217 yd [210 m]/25 g): #579 Splendour (purple; MC) and #597 Jelly (green; CC1), 2 balls each; #592 Trance (turquoise; CC2) and #581 Meadow (light green; CC3), 1 ball each.

NEEDLES Size U.S. 6 (4 mm): domino needles (page 6). Adjust needle size if necessary to obtain the correct gauge.

NOTIONS Tapestry needle.

GAUGE 1 square measures 3½" by 3½" (9 by 9 cm) and 5" (12.5 cm) across the diagonal.

[techniques]

▸ knit squares and blocks (page 9)
▸ reading charts (page 10)
▸ join three blocks into a pouch (page 60)
▸ weave in tails as you knit (page 12)
▸ see Glossary (page 133) for abbreviations and highlighted terms

[notes]

▸ To make a three-dimensional model of the cape, make a photocopy of the chart, cut it out, and tape it together so that Squares 10 and 17 (right shoulder) fit into the notches between Squares 4, 11, and 18 of the right front, and Squares 9, 16, and 23 of the back, and so that Squares 37 and 44 (left shoulder) fit into the notches between Squares 32, 38, and 45 of the back and Squares 36, 43, and 50 of the left front.
▸ Work the squares in garter stitch in numerical order in the colors specified (indicated by letters) on the chart. The direction of the numbers on the chart indicates the knitting direction.
▸ Work the cast-ons and bind-offs very loosely.

chapter four
join four blocks into a square

Join four blocks to form a large square that becomes the basis for a cap, afghan, or tote. The sample blocks shown here consist of nine squares (three panels of three squares each). Each square begins with 25 stitches and is worked in garter stitch. Diffferent colors are used here so the individual squares are easy to see.

BLOCKS 1 AND 2

Knit and join Squares 1 to 9
(Block 1) and Squares 10 to 18
(Block 2) as described on page
20, working each square in a
solid color.

BLOCK 3

Rotate joined Blocks 1 and 2 counterclockwise 90 degrees so that
Squares 18, 17, and 16 are at the top. Work nine squares for Block
3 along the right edge of Block 2 as follows.

PANEL 1
‹ Square 19
K-CO 13 sts, then **pick-knit** 12 sts along the right edge of
Square 10 (1 st in each CO loop)—25 sts total.
Row 1: (WS) Knit to the last st, p1 (**edge st**).
Row 2: (RS) Sl 1 kwise (edge st), k10, **sl 1 kwise, k2tog, psso,**
k10, p1 (edge st)—23 sts.
Row 3: Sl 1 kwise, knit to the last st, p1.
Row 4: Sl 1 kwise, knit to 1 st before the center st (i.e., k9), sl
1 kwise, k2tog, psso, knit to the last st (i.e., k9), p1—21 sts.
Row 5: Sl 1 kwise, knit to the last st, p1.
Rep Rows 4 and 5 until 3 sts rem on a RS row.
Next row: (WS) Sl 1, k1, p1.
Next row: Sl 1 kwise, k2tog, psso—1 st rem (**end st**). Leave
this st on the needle.

< Squares 20 and 21
Work as for Squares 11 and 12, pick-knitting sts along the right edge of Squares 13 and 16.

PANELS 2 AND 3
< Squares 22 to 27
Work as for Squares 13 to 18.

BLOCK 4
Rotate piece 90 degrees counterclockwise so that Squares 27, 26, and 25 are at the top. Work nine squares for Block 4 across the top of Block 1 and along the right edge of Block 3 as follows.

PANEL 1
< Square 28
Working from right to left, pick-knit 12 sts along the top of Square 1 (1 st in each CO loop), 1 st in the tip of Square 10, and 12 sts along the right edge of Square 19 (1 st in each CO loop)—25 sts total. Work as for Square 19.

‹ *Squares 29 and 30*
Work as for Squares 11 and 12, pick-knitting sts along the right edge of Squares 22 and 25.

PANELS 2 AND 3
‹ *Squares 31 to 36*
Work as for Squares 13 to 18.

four-block cap

The top of this tam-like cap is four four-square blocks (each consisting of two panels of two squares each) that are joined together to form a large square shape for the crown. The individual blocks are worked in different directions so that the decrease lines (and therefore, garter ridges) radiate out from the center point where the four blocks meet. You could substitute a single sixteen-square block for the center section, but you'd lose the attractive radiating pattern. A single square worked along the center two squares of each edge of the crown piece create the three-dimensional shape. Additional squares are added in rounds to give length to the sides, and the resulting gaps are filled in with triangles to produce a straight lower edge, which is finished with a ribbed or hemmed border.

[materials]

FINISHED SIZE About 23½ (25¼, 26¾)" (60 [64, 68] cm) in circumference. ***Squares with Dots Cap*** shown measures 22¾" (58 cm). ***Squares with Frames Cap*** shown measures 26½" (68 cm). ***Note:*** The exact size depends on the type of yarn and the size of the squares. If the cap is too loose, work a tight edging.

YARN Fingering weight (#1 Super Fine) in a main color and 3 or 4 contrasting colors.

Shown here: Harrisville New England Knitter's Shetland (100% wool; 217 yd [200 m]/50 g). ***Squares with Dots Cap:*** Hyacinth (MC), 1 skein; Lilac, Tundra, Cornflower, and Seagreen, less than 1 skein each. ***Squares with Frames Cap:*** Blackberry (MC), 1 skein; Plum, Magenta, and Poppy, less than 1 skein each.

NEEDLES Size 3 mm (between U.S. 2 and 3): domino needles (page 6). Edging—size 2.5 mm (between U.S. 1 and 2): 16" (40 cm) circular (cir). Adjust needle size if necessary to obtain the correct gauge.

NOTIONS Tapestry needle; marker (m).

GAUGE 1 square measures about 2 by 2 (2¼ by 2¼, 2½ by 2½)" (5 by 5 [5.5 by 5.5, 6 by 6] cm) and 3 (3⅛, 3¼)" (7.5 [8,8.5] cm) along the diagonal. To fit adult small (medium, large).

[techniques]

- knit squares and blocks (page 9)
- reading charts (page 10)
- join four blocks into a square (page 82)
- weave in tails as you knit (page 12)
- see Glossary (page 133) for abbreviations and highlighted terms

[notes]

▼ To make a three-dimensional model of the cap, make a photocopy of the chart, cut it out, and tape it together connecting Squares 17 and 33 to Squares 2 and 24; Squares 18 and 35 to Squares 6 and 26; Squares 19 and 29 to Squares 10 and 28; and Squares 20 and 31 to Squares 14 and 22.

▼ Work the squares and triangles in numerical order specified on the chart and colors indicated on page 89. The direction of the numbers on the chart indicates the knitting direction.

▼ The four basic blocks are shaded on the chart.

BLOCK 1
PANEL 1
‹ *Square 1*

With the color specified, **K-CO** 25 (27, 29) sts. Changing colors as specified for your cap on page 89, work in garter st as foll:

Row 1: (WS) Knit to the last st, p1.

Row 2: (RS) Sl 1 kwise (**edge st**), knit to 1 st before center st, **sl 1 kwise, k2tog, psso**, knit to last st, p1 (edge st)—2 sts decreased.

Row 3: Sl 1 kwise (edge st), knit to last st, p1 (edge st).

Rep Rows 2 and 3 until 3 sts rem on a RS row.

Next row: (WS) Sl 1 kwise, k1, p1.

Next row: (RS) Sl 1 kwise, k2tog, psso—1 st rem (**end st**).

‹ *Square 2*

Using the end st from Square 1 as the first st of Square 2, **pick-knit** 11 (12, 13) sts along the upper edge of Square 1 (**Note**: Skip the first edge st because the end st from Square 1 is now the first st of Square 2; it doesn't matter that it's a different color), go **"around the corner"** and pick-knit 1 st in the nearest CO loop, **turn work,** and K-CO 12 (13, 14) new sts—25 (27, 29) sts total. Work as for Square 1 but end by pulling the end st loose, cutting the yarn, and threading the tail through it.

PANEL 2
‹ *Square 3*

K-CO 12 (13, 14) sts, hold the previous block of Squares in your left hand with RS facing and the needle with the K-CO sts in your right hand, pick-knit 11 (12, 13) sts along the right edge of Square 1 and 1 st in the end st of Square 4 (pull the end-st tail tight to secure this st)—25 (27, 29) sts

total. Work as for Square 1 but beg the first row with sl 1 pwise with yarn in front (wyf).

‹ *Square 4*

Using the end st from Square 3 as the first st of Square 4, pick-knit 11 (12, 13) sts along the upper edge of Square 3, 1 st in the tip of Squares 1 and 12 (13, 14) sts along right edge of Square 2—25 (27, 29) sts total. Work as for Square 1 but beg the first row with sl 1 pwise wyf. End by pulling the end st loose, cutting the yarn, and threading the tail through it.

BLOCK 2

Rotate Block 1 so that Squares 4 and 3 are at the top.

‹ *Square 5*

K-CO 12 (13, 14) sts. Hold the previous block of Squares in your left hand with RS facing and the needle with the K-CO sts in your right hand, then pick-knit 1 st "around the corner" *under* Square 1 in the center CO loop, then pick-knit 12 (13, 14) sts along the left edge of Square 1—25 (27, 29) sts total. Work as for Square 1 but beg the first row with sl 1 pwise wyf.

‹ *Squares 6, 7, and 8*

Foll the placement specified on the chart, work as for Squares 2, 3, and 4 of Block 1.

BLOCK 3

Rotate the piece so that Squares 8 and 7 are at the top.

‹ *Squares 9, 10, 11, and 12*

Foll the placement specified on the chart, work as for Squares 5, 6, 7, and 8 of Block 2.

BLOCK 4

Rotate the piece so that Squares 12 and 11 are at the top.

COLOR KEY

Squares with Dots: K-CO or pick-knit with the main color (MC), continue with MC until 11 sts rem, work to end with specified contrast color.

Lilac: Squares 1, 7, 9, 15, 22, 24, 26, and 28.

Tundra: Squares 2, 6, 10, 14, 21, and 25.

Seagreen: Squares 3, 5, 11, 13, 23, and 27.

Cornflower: Squares 4, 8, 12, 16, and 17 to 20.

Squares with Frames: Work the initial CO or pick-knit row with the main color (MC), continue with MC for 3 more rows, work to end with specified contrast color.

Poppy: Squares 1, 4, 8, 9, 12, 16, 17, 18, 19, and 20.

Plum: Squares 2, 6, 7, 11, 13, and 21 to 28.

Magenta: Squares 3, 5, 10, 14, and 15.

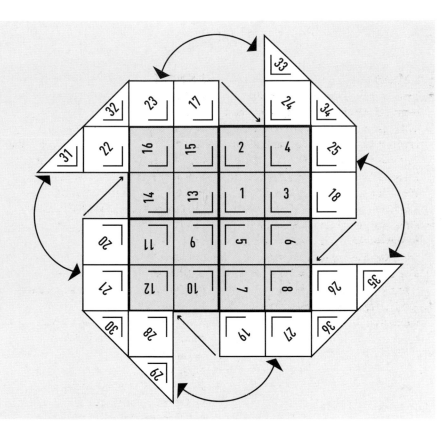

PANEL 1

‹ *Square 13*

Working from right to left, pick-knit 12 sts along Square 1 (1 st in each CO loop), 1 st in the tip of Square 5, and 12 sts along the right edge of Square 9—25 sts total. Work as for Square 19.

‹ *Square 14*

Work as for Square 13, pick-knitting sts along the upper edge of Square 13, 1 between Squares 9 and 11, and along Square 11.

PANEL 2

‹ *Squares 15 and 16*

Work as for Squares 11 to 12.

JOIN SQUARES FOR THREE-DIMENSIONAL SHAPE

‹ *Square 17*

Pick-knit 25 (27, 29) sts along Squares 2 and 15, pick-knitting the center st between Squares 2 and 15. Work as for Square 1 but beg the first row with sl 1 pwise wyf. **BO** the end st.

‹ *Squares 18, 19, and 20*

Foll the placement specified on the chart, work as for Square 17.

ADD LENGTH IN ROUNDS

ROUND 1

‹ *Square 21*

Pick-knit 12 (13, 14) sts along the upper left edge of Square 20, 1 st in the tip of Square 11, and 12 (13, 14) sts along the right edge of Square 12 (ending just before the end st of Square 12)—25 (27, 29) sts total. Work as for Square 1 but beg the first row with sl 1 pwise wyf. BO the end st.

‹ *Squares 22 to 28*

Foll the placement specified on the chart, join the yarn, pick-knit 12 (13, 14) sts along both edges of adjoining squares as shown, then work as for Square 21.

ROUND 2

Work triangles in the notches between the last round of squares as follows.

‹ *Triangle 29*

Pick-knit 12 (13, 14) sts along the left edge of Square 28, 1 st in the tip of Square 19, and 12 (13, 14) sts along the right edge of Square 27—25 (27, 29) sts total.

Row 1: (WS) Sl 1 pwise wyf, knit to last st, p1.

Row 2: (RS) Sl 1 kwise, **ssk,** k8 (9, 10), sl 1 kwise, k2tog, psso, k8 (9, 10), **k2tog,** p1—21 (23, 25) sts.

Row 3 and all foll WS rows: Sl 1 kwise, knit to last st, p1.

Row 4: Sl 1 kwise, ssk, k6 (7, 8), sl 1 kwise, k2tog, psso, k6 (7, 8), k2tog, p1—17 (19, 21) sts.

Row 6: Sl 1 kwise, ssk, k4 (5, 6), sl 1 kwise, k2tog, psso, k4 (7, 8), k2tog, p1—13 (15, 17) sts.

Row 8: Sl 1 kwise, ssk, k2 (3, 4), sl 1 kwise, k2tog, psso, k2 (3, 4), k2tog, p1—9 (11, 13) sts.

Row 10: Sl 1 kwise, ssk, k0 (1, 2), sl 1 kwise, k2tog, psso, k0 (1, 2), k2tog, p1—5 (7, 9) sts.

SIZE SMALL ONLY:

Row 12: Sl 1 kwise (edge st), sl 1 kwise, k2tog, psso, pl—3 sts.

Row 13: (WS) Sl 1 kwise, k2tog, psso—1 st rem. BO the end st.

SIZE MEDIUM ONLY:

Row 12: Sl 1 kwise, k1, sl 1 kwise, k2tog, psso, k1, p1—5 sts.

Row 14: Sl 1 kwise (edge st), sl 1 kwise, k2tog, psso, pl—3 sts.

Row 15: (WS) Sl 1 kwise, k2tog, psso—1 st rem. BO the end st.

SIZE LARGE ONLY:

Row 12: Sl 1 kwise, ssk, sl 1 kwise, k2tog, psso, p1—5 sts.

Row 14: Sl 1 kwise (edge st), sl 1 kwise, k2tog, psso, p1—3 sts.

Row 15: (WS) Sl 1 kwise, k2tog, psso—1 st rem. BO the end st.

‹ *Triangles 30 to 36*

Foll the placement specified on the chart, work as for Triangle 29.

FINISHING

Weave in loose ends. Choose the edging of your choice.

RIBBED EDGING

With cir needle and RS facing, pick-knit 10 (11, 11) sts in each square around cap opening—80 (88, 88) sts total. Work k1, p1 rib for 24 rnds or to desired length. BO all sts loosely as foll: *BO 2 sts, slip the rem st to left needle and knit it again; rep from * until all sts have been BO.

HEMMED EDGING

With cir needle and RS facing, pick-knit 108 sts evenly spaced around the lower edge. Purl 1 rnd. Knit 8 rnds. Purl 1 rnd for turning ridge, then knit 7 more rnds. BO all sts loosely. Fold the edging to the WS along turning ridge and with yarn threaded on a tapestry needle, sew in place.

afghan

This colorful afghan, contributed by Norwegian designer Margit Henriksen, shows how easy it is to join four blocks into a large rectangle. Instead of working the same number of squares across the base of the block as along the height, Margit simply added more panels or added more squares to the panels to give each block a rectangular shape. Two of the blocks consist of fourteen panels of eight squares each; two consist of eight panels of fourteen squares each. Because the blocks are rotated with respect to one another, the decrease lines (and garter ridges) radiate out from the center point where the four blocks meet. The color pattern shown here was carefully designed to grade from light to dark to light, but you could just as easily use leftover yarns and let serendipity be your guide.

[materials]

FINISHED SIZE
About 36¼" (92 cm) wide and 64¼" (163 cm) long, including I-cord border.

YARN Fingering weight (#1 Super Fine) in 13 colors.
Shown here: Rauma Finullgarn 7/2 (100% wool; 191 yd [175 m]/ 50 g): #450 Light Yellow, #461 Orange, #445 Dark Red, #424 Red, #465 Pink, #484 Dark Turquoise, #483 Turquoise, #455 Grassy Green, #454 Lime, #496 Medium Violet, #4088 Lilac, #442 Blue Violet, and #448 Bright Navy Blue. Calculate the amount of each color by knitting a couple of squares and weigh them to determine the weight of yarn required for the number of squares worked in each color, allowing a little extra for tails: 8 Light Yellow; 16 Orange; 24 Dark Red; 32 Red; 40 Pink; 48 Dark Turquoise; 40 Turquoise; 32 Grassy Green; 24 Lime; 16 Medium Violet; 8 Lilac; 76 Blue Violet; 80 Bright Navy Blue, plus I-cord border.

NEEDLES Size 2.5 or 3 mm (U.S. size 2): domino needles (page 6) plus two double-pointed needles (dpn) 1 size larger. Adjust needle size if necessary to obtain the correct gauge.
NOTIONS Tapestry needle.
GAUGE Each square measures 2.4" by 2.4" (6 by 6) cm.

[techniques]

▸ knit squares and blocks (page 9)
▸ reading charts (page 10)
▸ join four blocks into a square (page 82)
▸ See Glossary (page 133) for abbreviations and highlighted terms.

[notes]

▸ Work the squares in numerical order and in the colors specified on the chart.
▸ An I-cord edging is added to the completed squares.

BLOCK 1
PANEL 1
‹ *Square 1*

With Light Yellow, **K-CO** 25 sts.

Row 1: (WS) Knit to the last st, p1 (**edge st**).

Row 2: (RS) Sl 1 kwise (edge st), knit to center st (i.e, k10), sl 1 **kwise, k2tog, psso, k10,** p1 (**edge st**).

Row 3: Sl 1 kwise, knit to last st, p1.

Row 4: Sl 1 kwise, knit to 1 st before the center st (i.e., k9), sl 1 kwise, k2tog, psso, knit to the last st, p1—21 sts.

Row 5: Sl 1 kwise, knit to last st, p1. Rep Rows 4 and 5 until 3 sts rem on a RS row.

Next row: (WS) Sl 1 kwise, k1, p1.

Next row: Sl 1 kwise, k2tog, psso—1 st rem (end st). Cut yarn.

‹ *Square 2*

Using the end st from Square 1 as the first st of Square 2, with Orange **pick-knit** 11 more sts along the upper edge of Square 1 (**Note:** Skip the first edge st because the end st from Square 1 is now the first st of Square 2; it doesn't matter that it's a different color), go **"around the corner"** and pick-knit 1 st in the nearest CO loop, **turn work,** and K-CO 12 new sts—25 sts total. Work as for Square 1 but beg the first row with sl 1 pwise with yarn in front (wyf).

‹ *Squares 3 to 8*

With colors specified on the chart, work as for Square 2, always pick-knitting sts along the upper edge of the square just completed.

PANEL 2
‹ *Square 9*

With Orange, K-CO 12 sts. Hold the first panel of Squares 1–8 in your left hand with RS facing and the needle with the K-CO sts in your right hand, pick-knit 1 st "around the corner" under Square 1 in the far right CO loop, then pick-knit 12 sts along the right edge of Square 1—25 sts total. Work as for Square 1 but beg the first row with sl 1 pwise wyf.

‹ *Square 10*

Using the end st from Square 9 as the first st of Square 10, with Dark Red pick-knit 11 more sts along the upper edge of Square 9, 1 st in the upper right tip of Square 1 (by the end st), and 12 sts along Square 2—25 sts total. Work as for Square 1 but beg the first row with sl 1 pwise wyf.

‹ *Squares 11 to 16*

Foll the the sequence and colors indicated on the chart, work as for Square 10, always beg at the top of the square just completed.

PANELS 3 TO 14

Foll the sequence and colors indicated on the chart, work as for Panel 2.

BLOCK 2

Rotate the piece just worked counterclockwise so that Squares 105 to 112 are along the top edge.

PANEL 1
‹ *Square 113*

With Light Yellow, K-CO 13 sts. Hold the previous block of squares in your left hand with RS facing and the needle with the K-CO sts in your right hand, then pick-knit 12 sts along the right edge of Square 1—25 sts total. Work as for Square 1 but beg the first row with sl 1 pwise wyf.

‹ *Square 114*

Using the end st from Square 113 as the first st of Square 114, pick-knit 11 more sts along the upper edge of Square 113, 1 st between Squares 1 and 9, and 12 sts along the right edge of Square 9—25 sts. Work as for Square 1 but beg the first row with sl 1 pwise wyf.

‹ Squares 115 to 126

Foll the sequence and colors indicated on the chart, work as for Square 114, always beg at the top of the square just completed.

PANELS 2 TO 8

Foll the sequence and colors indicated on the chart, work as for Panels 2 to 8 of Block 1.

BLOCK 3

Rotate the piece just worked counterclockwise so that Squares 211 to 224 are along the top edge.

PANEL 1

‹ Square 225

With Light Yellow, K-CO 13 sts. Hold the previous block of Squares in your left hand with RS facing and the needle with the K-CO sts in your right hand, then pick-knit 12 sts along the right edge of Square 113—25 sts total. Work as for Square 1 but beg the first row with sl 1 pwise wyf.

‹ Square 226

Using the end st from Square 225 as the first st of Square 226, pick-knit 11 more sts along the upper edge of Square 225, 1 st between Squares 113 and 127, and 12 sts along the right edge of Square 127—25 sts total. Work as for Square 1 but beg the first row with sl 1 pwise wyf.

Color key:

- Light Yellow
- Orange
- Dark Red
- Red
- Pink
- Dark Turquoise
- Turquoise
- Grassy Green
- Lime
- Medium Violet
- Lilac
- Blue Violet
- Bright Navy Blue

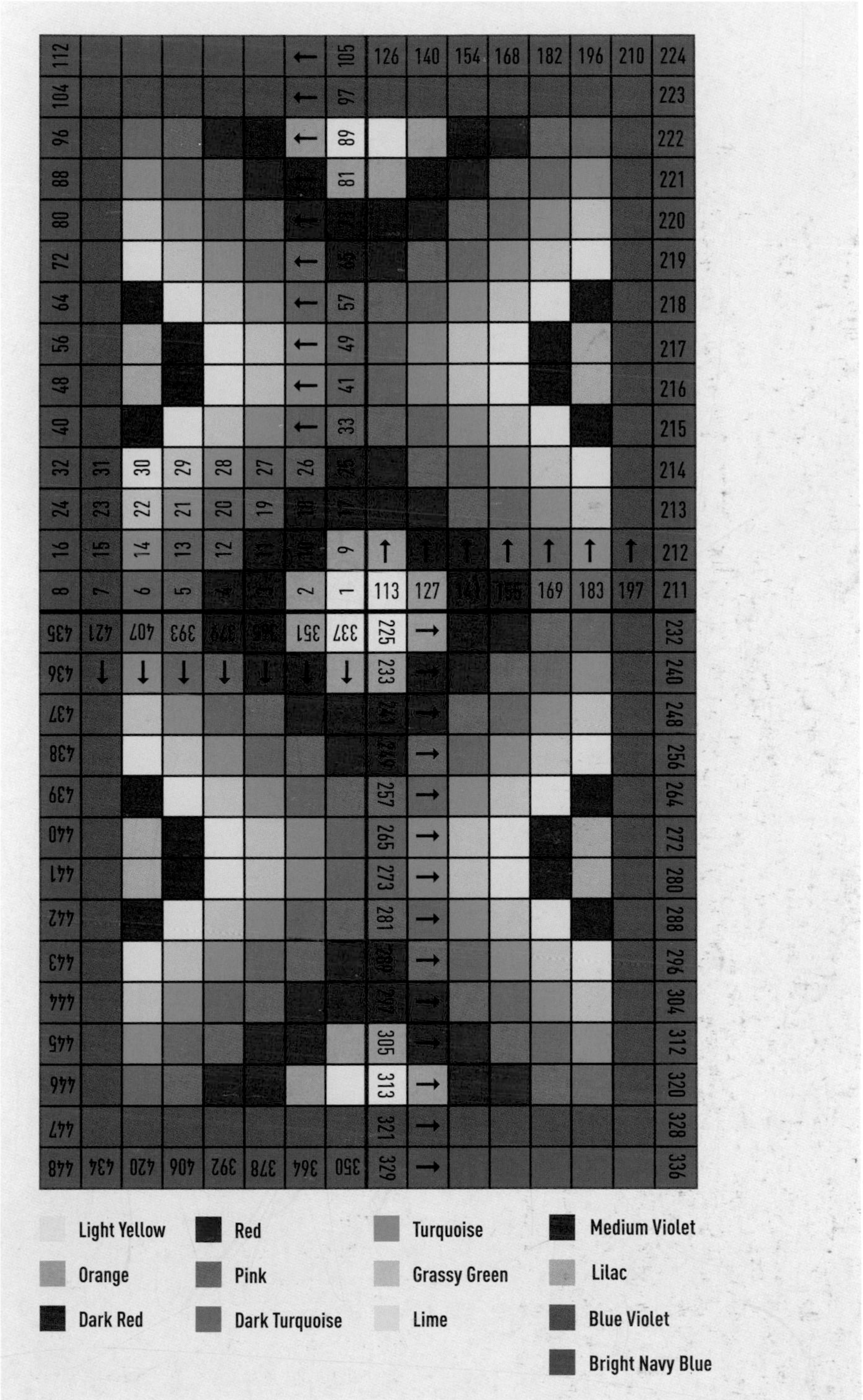

< *Squares 227 to 232*

Foll the sequence and colors indicated on the chart, work as for Square 226, always beg at the top of the square just completed.

PANELS 2 TO 14

Foll the sequence and colors indicated on the chart, work as for Panels 2 to 14 of Block 1.

BLOCK 4

Rotate the piece just worked counterclockwise so that Squares 329 to 336 are along the top edge.

PANEL 1

< *Square 337*

With Light Yellow, pick-knit 12 sts along top edge of Square 1 (1 st in each CO loop), 1 st in the tip of Square 113, and 12 sts along the right edge of Square 225—25 sts total. Work as for Square 1 but beg the first row with sl 1 pwise wyf.

< *Squares 338 to 350*

Foll the sequence and colors indicated on the chart, work as for Square 337, always beg at the top of the square just completed and joining each square to Block 3.

PANELS 2 TO 8

Foll the sequence and colors indicated on the chart, work as for Panels 2 to 8 of Block 1, beg each panel along the upper edge of Block 1.

FINISHING

Weave in loose ends.

I-CORD EDGING

With Bright Navy Blue, double-pointed needles, and RS facing, using the end sl from Square as the first st 1 st in upper right corner of last afghan square worked, then K-CO 4 new sts—5 sts total on needle. Work *I-cord* BO as foll: K3, *p2tog* (the last CO st and the pick-knitted st). *Bring the yarn behind the work, pick-knit under both loops of the next edge st on the upper edge of the afghan from WS to RS, pull the yarn tight behind the work, slide the sts to the far end of dpn, k3, *k2tog* (1 st from the edging and the double loop from the afghan). Rep from * around the entire circumference of the afghan, working 3 to 5 rows of unattached I-cord at each corner. *BO* all sts. With yarn threaded on a tapestry needle, sew BO edge to CO edge as invisibly as possible. Block lightly.

bucket bag

This roomy bag is constructed like the Four-Block Cap on page 86, but in this case, the initial four blocks form the bag base instead of the cap top. Additional squares are worked around the four-block base to form the cup shape and add length to the sides. To give the bag it's distinctive zigzag edge, the gaps between the squares are left as they are; they are not filled in with triangles. To provide holes for attaching the straps (which are simply two leather belts), the final round of squares are bound off when thirteen stitches remain. The edging is picked up around the upper edge and shaped with well-placed increases and decreases. After felting, the bag is shaped over an upside-down bucket.

[materials]

FINISHED SIZE Before felting: About 30¾" (78 cm) around and 17" (43 cm) tall, including edging. After felting: About 24½" (62 cm) around and 13.4" (34 cm) tall, including edging. **Note:** The final measurements depend on the size of the bucket used for blocking.

YARN Fingering weight (#1 Super Fine) in 5 colors.

Shown here: Harrisville New England Knitter's Shetland (100% wool; 217 yd [200 m]/50 g): Hyacinth (A), Iris (B), Periwinkle (C), Magenta (D), and Tundra (E), 1 skein each.

NEEDLES Size U.S. 4 or 6 (3.5 or 4 mm): domino needles (page 6) and 24" (60 cm) circular (cir). Adjust needle size if necessary to obtain the correct gauge.

NOTIONS Tapestry needle; two ½" (1.3 cm) belts, each about 44" (112 cm) long.

GAUGE Before felting:1 square measures about 2¾" by 2¾" (6.9 by 6.9 cm) and 3.8" (9.8 cm) along the diagonal. After felting: 1 square measures about 2.2" by 2.2" (5.5 by 5.5 cm) and 3" (7.8 cm) along the diagonal.

[techniques]

◣ knit squares and blocks (page 9)
◣ reading charts (page 10)
◣ join four blocks into a square (page 82)
◣ weave in tails as you knit (page 12)
◣ see Glossary (page 133) for abbreviations and highlighted terms

[notes]

▼ To make a three-dimensional model of the bag, make a photocopy of the chart, cut it out, and tape it together connecting Squares 17, 33, and 52 to Squares 2, 24, 42, and 43; Squares 18, 35, and 46 to Squares 6, 26, 44, and 37; Squares 19, 29, and 48 to Squares 10, 28, and 39; and Squares 20, 31, and 50 to Squares 14, 22, and 41.

▼ Work the squares in numerical order and colors (indicated by letters) specified on the chart. The direction of the numbers on the chart indicates the knitting direction.

▼ The four basic blocks are shaded on the chart.

BLOCK 1
PANEL 1
‹ *Square 1*

With Tundra, **K-CO** 31 sts. Work in garter st, changing colors as foll:

Row 1: (WS) Knit to the last st, p1 (**edge st**).

Row 2: (RS) Change to Hyacinth. Sl 1 kwise (edge st), knit to 1 st before center sl (i.e., k13), **sl 1 kwise, k2tog, psso,** knit to last st (i.e., k13), p1 (edge st)—2 sts decreased.

Row 3: Sl 1 kwise, knit to last st, p1.

Rep Rows 2 and 3 until 3 sts rem on a RS row, changing to Iris on Row 20.

Next row: (WS) Sl 1 kwise, k1, p1.

Next row: (RS) Sl 1 kwise, k2tog, psso—1 st rem (**end st**).

‹ *Square 2*

Using the end st from Square 1 as the first st of Square 2, with Tundra, **pick-knit** 15 sts along the upper edge of Square 1 (**Note:** Skip the first edge st because the end st from Square 1 is now the first st of Square 2; it doesn't matter that it's a different color), go **"around the corner"** and pick-knit 1 st in the nearest CO loop, **turn work,** and K-CO 15 new sts—31 sts total. Work as for Square 1, changing colors as specified for color sequence for C, and ending by pulling the end st loose, cutting the yarn, and threading the tail through it.

PANEL 2
‹ *Square 3*

With Tundra, K-CO 15 sts. Hold the previous block of Squares in your left hand with RS facing and the needle with the K-CO sts in your right hand, then pick-knit 1 st "around the corner" *under* Square 1 in the far right CO loop, and 15 sts along the right edge of Square 1—31 sts total. Work as for Square 1 but beg the first row with sl 1

pwise with yarn in front (wyf) and change colors as specified for color sequence C.

‹ *Square 4*

Using the end st from Square 3 as the first st of Square 4, with Tundra, pick-knit 14 sts along the upper edge of Square 3, 1 st in the tip of Square 1, 14 sts along right edge of Square 2, and 1 st in the end st of Square 2—31 sts total. Work as for Square 1 but beg the first row with sl 1 pwise wyf, change colors as specified for color sequence D. **BO** the end st.

BLOCK 2

Rotate Block 1 so that Squares 4 and 3 are at the top.

‹ *Square 5*

With Tundra, K-CO 16 sts. Hold the previous block of squares in your left hand with RS facing and the needle with the K-CO sts in your right hand, then pick-knit 15 sts along the left edge of Square 1—31 sts total. Work as for Square 1 but beg the first row with sl 1 pwise wyf and change colors as specified for color sequence A.

‹ *Squares 6, 7, and 8*

Foll the placement and colors specified on the chart, work as for Squares 2, 3, and 4 of Block 1.

BLOCK 3

Rotate the piece so that Squares 8 and 7 are at the top.

‹ *Squares 9 to 12*

Foll the placement and colors specified on the chart, work as for Squares 5, 6, 7, and 8 of Block 2.

BLOCK 4

Rotate the piece so that Squares 12 and 11 are at the top.

COLOR SEQUENCE

A: K-CO or pick-knit sts and work 1 row with Tundra; work next 18 rows with Iris; work to end with Hyacinth.

B: K-CO or pick-knit sts and work 1 row with Tundra; work next 18 rows with Hyacinth; work to end with Iris.

C: K-CO or pick-knit sts and work 1 row with Tundra; work next 18 rows with Periwinkle; work to end with Iris.

D: K-CO or pick-knit sts and work 1 row of Tundra; work next 18 rows with Hyacinth; work to end with Magenta.

E: K-CO or pick-knit sts and work 1 row with Tundra; work next 18 rows with Periwinkle; work to end with Hyacinth.

G: Pick-knit sts and work 1 row with Tundra; work next 18 rows with Iris; work to end with Magenta.

H: K-CO or pick-knit sts and work 1 row with Tundra; work to end with Hyacinth.

52/H
51/H 42/C 33/G
41/C 32/G 23/E 17/D   24/E 34/G 44/C 46/H
                              43/C 45/H
22/E 16/D 15/C 2/C 4/D 25/E 35/G
      14/C 13/A 1/B 3/C 18/D
20/D 11/C 9/B 5/A 6/C
31/G 21/E 12/D 10/C 7/C 8/D 26/E
50/H 40/C 30/G 28/E 19/D 27/E 36/G 37/C
49/H 39/C 29/G 38/C 47/H
48/H

‹ *Squares 13 to 16*

Foll the placement and colors specified on the chart, work as for Squares 5, 6, 7, and 8 of Block 2 but pick-knit the center st of Square 13 in the tip of Square 5.

JOIN SQUARES FOR THREE-DIMENSIONAL SHAPE

‹ *Square 17*

With Tundra, pick-knit 31 sts along Squares 2 and 15, pick-knitting the center st between Squares 2 and 15. Work as for Square 1, following color sequence D. BO the end st.

‹ *Squares 18, 19, and 20*

Foll the placement and colors specified on the chart, work as for Square 17 but do not BO the end st of Square 20.

ADD LENGTH IN ROUNDS

ROUND 1

‹ *Square 21*

With Tundra, pick-knit 15 sts across the left edge of Square 20, 1 st in the tip of Square 11, and 15 sts along the right edge of Square 12—31 sts total. Work as for Square 1, following color sequence E. BO the end st.

‹ *Square 22*

With Tundra, pick-knit 15 sts along the left edge of Square 16, 1 st in the tip of Square 14, and 15 sts along the left edge of Square 20—31 sts total. Work as for Square 21, following color sequence E.

‹ *Squares 23 to 28*

Foll the placement and colors specified on the chart, working K-CO and/or pick-knitting sts as indicated on chart, work as for Square 21.

ROUND 2

‹ *Squares 29 to 36*

Foll the placement and colors specified on the chart, working K-CO and/or pick-knitting sts as indicated on chart, work as for Square 21.

ROUND 3

‹ *Squares 37 to 44*

Foll the placement and colors specified on the chart, working K-CO and/or pick-knitting sts as indicated on chart, work as for Square 21.

ROUND 4

‹ *Squares 45 to 52*

Foll the placement and colorway H as specified on the chart, work as for Square 22, but when 13 sts rem, BO on the next RS row and *at the same time* knit the first st (do not slip it) and work a double decrease on the center 3 sts as usual.

FINISHING

Weave in loose ends.

ZIGZAG EDGING

With Tundra, cir needle, RS facing, and beg at the boundary between Squares 51 and 52, *pick-knit 1 st at the tip of Square 42, 10 sts along the right edge of Square 51, turn work, K-CO 8 sts, turn work again, pick knit 10 sts along the left side of Square 51; rep from * across Squares 50, 49, 48, 47, 46, 45, and 52—232 sts total.

Rnd 1: Purl.

Rnd 2: Change to Iris. Sl the first 2 sts, *k12, *M1* (lift the horizontal strand between the needles and knit it through the back loop), k2, M1, k12, sl 1 kwise with yarn in back (wyb), k2tog, psso *; rep from *—2 sts increased and decreased per patt rep.

Rnd 3: Purl.

Rnds 4–9: Rep Rnds 2 and 3 three more times.

Rnds 10 and 11: Change to Tundra. Rep Rnds 3 and 4. Loosely BO all sts.

FELTING AND SHAPING

Felt the piece in the washing machine according to the guildines on page 137. Stretch the wet bag over the top of an upside-down bucket of suitable size. Allow the bag to thoroughly air-dry, stretching it periodically, before removing it from the bucket.

STRAPS

Cut the leather belts to the desired length, allowing 2½" (6.5 cm) hem at each end. Insert each end of each belt through a hole below the edging, fold the end up about 2½" (6.5 cm), and use a sewing machine to securely stitch in place.

rosebud duffel

Beginning with a four-block base (each block consisting of two panels of two squares each), this generous tote follows the same initial construction as the Bucket Bag on page 98, but the piece is lengthened with a few more rounds of additional squares and the sides extend into points at the top. The base is worked in solid black, but the squares along the side end with a narrow band of green followed by a bright contrasting color. Even though these colors are knitted as stripes, they form isolated "rosebud" motifs. The edging and strap are worked in two sections, then the bag is felted in the washing machine. If desired, the bag can be lined with commercial fabric.

[materials]

FINISHED SIZE Before felting: About 36½" (93 cm) around and 30" (76 cm) long, including edging. After felting: About 29¼" (74 cm) around and 24" (61 cm) long, including edging.

YARN Fingering weight (#1 Super Fine) in 1 main color and 4 contrasting colors.

Shown here: Harrisville New England Knitter's Shetland (100% wool; 217 yd [200 m]/50 g): Black, 6 skeins; Tundra, Poppy, Red, and Magenta, 1 skein each.

NEEDLES Size U.S. 4 or 6 (3.5 or 4 mm): domino needles (page 6) and 24" (60 cm) circular (cir). Adjust needle size if necessary to obtain the correct gauge.

NOTIONS Tapestry needle; about 1 yd (91.5 cm) cotton fabric for lining; sharp-point sewing needle and matching thread for attaching lining.

GAUGE Before felting: 1 square measures about 3¼" by 3¼" (8.2 by 8.2 cm) and 4½" (11.6 cm) across the diagonal. After felting: 1 square measures about 2½" by 2½" (6.6 by 6.6 cm) and 3¾" (9.3 cm) across the diagonal.

[techniques]

▼ knit squares and blocks (page 9)
▼ reading charts (page 10)
▼ join four blocks into a square (page 82)
▼ weave in tails as you knit (page 12)
▼ see Glossary (page 133) for abbreviations and highlighted terms

[notes]

▶ To make a three-dimensional model of the bag, make a photocopy of the chart, cut it out, and tape it together connecting Squares 17, 32, 51, and 61 to Squares 2, 23, 42, and 53; Squares 18, 34, 45, and 63 to Squares 6, 25, 44, and 55; Squares 19, 36, 47, and 67 to Squares 10, 27, 38, and 57; and Squares 20, 30, 49, and 69 to Squares 14, 21, 40, and 59.

▶ Work the squares in numerical order and colors (indicated by letters) specified on the chart. The direction of the numbers on the chart indicates the knitting direction.

▶ The four basic blocks are shaded on the chart.

BLOCK 1

PANEL 1

‹ *Square 1*

With Black, **K-CO** 37 sts. Work in garter st as foll:

Row 1: (WS) Knit to the last st, p1 (**edge st**).

Row 2: (RS) Sl 1 kwise (edge st), knit to 1 st before center st (i.e., k16), **sl 1 kwlse, k2tog, psso,** knit to last st (i.e., k16), p1 (edge st).

Row 3: Sl 1 kwise (edge st), knit to last st, p1 (edge st).

Rep Rows 2 and 3 until 3 sts rem on a RS row.

Next row: (WS) Sl 1 kwise, k1, p1.

Next row: (RS) Sl 1 kwise, k2tog, psso—1 st rem (**end st**).

‹ *Square 2*

Using the end st from Square 1 as the first st of Square 2, with Black, **pick-knit** 17 sts along the upper edge of Square 1, go **"around the corner"** and pick-knit 1 st in the nearest CO loop, **turn work,** and K-CO 18 new sts—37 sts total. Work as for Square 1 but pull the end st loose, cut the yarn, and thread the tail through it.

PANEL 2

‹ *Square 3*

With Black, K-CO 18 sts. Hold the previous block of squares in your left hand with RS facing and the needle with the K-CO sts in your right hand, then pick-knit 1 st "around the corner" *under* Square 1 in the far right CO loop, then pick-knit 18 sts along the right edge of Square 1—37 sts total. Work as for Square 1 but beg the first row with sl 1 pwise with yarn in front (wyf).

‹ *Square 4*

Using the end st from Square 3 as the first st of Square 4, with Black, pick-knit 17 sts along the upper edge of Square 3, 1 st in the tip of Square 1, 18 sts along right edge of Square 2, and 1 st in the end st of Square 2—37 sts total. Work as for Square 1 but beg the first row with sl 1 pwise wyf and change colors as specified for color sequence B. **BO** the end st.

BLOCK 2

Rotate Block 1 so that Squares 4 and 3 are at the top.

‹ *Square 5*

With Black, K-CO 19 sts. Hold the previous block of squares in your left hand with RS facing and the needle with the K-CO sts in your right hand, then pick-knit 18 sts along the left edge of Square 1—37 sts total. Work as for Square 1 but beg the first row with sl 1 pwise wyf.

‹ *Squares 6, 7, and 8*

Foll the placement and colors specified on the chart, work as for Squares 2, 3, and 4 of Block 1.

BLOCK 3

Rotate the piece so that Squares 8 and 7 are at the top.

‹ *Squares 9 to 12*

Foll the placement and colors specified on the chart, work as for Squares 5, 6, 7, and 8 of Block 2.

BLOCK 4

Rotate the piece so that Squares 12 and 11 are at the top.

‹ *Squares 13 to 16*

Foll the placement and colors specified on the chart, work as for Squares 5, 6, 7, and 8 of Block 2, pick-knitting all sts from adjacent squares as indicated on chart but pick-knit the center st of Square 13 in the tip of Square 5.

COLOR KEY

A: Black.

B: K-CO and/or pick-knit sts and work 15 rows with Black; work next 4 rows with Tundra; work to end with Red.

C: K-CO and/or pick-knit sts and work 15 rows with Black; work next 4 rows with Tundra; work to end with Poppy.

D: K-CO and/or pick-knit sts and work 15 rows with Black; work next 4 rows with Tundra; work to end with Magenta.

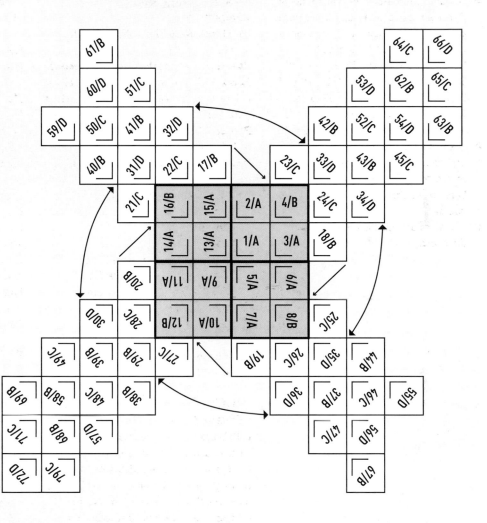

JOIN SQUARES FOR THREE-DIMENSIONAL SHAPE

‹ *Square 17*

With Black, pick-knit 31 sts along Squares 2 and 15, pick-knitting the center st between Squares 2 and 15. Work as for Square 1 but beg the first row with sl 1 pwise wyf and foll color sequence B. **BO** the end st.

‹ *Squares 18, 19, and 20*

Foll the placement and colors specified on the chart, work as for Square 17 but leave the end st of Square 20 on the needle.

ADD LENGTH IN ROUNDS

ROUND 1

‹ *Square 21*

With Black, pick-knit 18 sts along the upper edge of Square 16, 1 st in the tip of Square 14, and 18 sts along the right edge of Square 20—37 sts total. Work as for Square 1, but beg the first row with sl 1 pwise wyf and foll color sequence C. BO the end st.

‹ *Squares 22 to 28*

Foll the placement and colors specified on the chart, work as for Square 21.

ROUND 2

‹ *Squares 29 to 36*

Foll the placement and colors specified on the chart, work as for Square 21.

ROUND 3

‹ *Squares 37 to 44*

Foll the placement and colors sqecified on the chart, work as for Square 21.

ROUND 4

‹ *Squares 45 to 52*

Foll the placement and colors sqecified on the chart, work as for Square 21.

ROUND 5

‹ *Squares 53 to 60*

Foll the placement and colors sqecified on the chart, work as for Square 21.

EXTEND THE SIDES

RIGHT SIDE

‹ *Squares 61, 62, and 63*

Knit a square in each of the following 3 notches: 53-51-60, 54-52-53, and 55-45-54.

‹ *Squares 64 and 65*

Knit a square in each of the following 2 notches: 62-53-61 and 63-54-62.

‹ *Square 66*

Knit a square in notch 65-62-64.

LEFT SIDE

‹ *Squares 67 to 72*

Foll the placement and colors specified on the chart, work as for Right Side.

FINISHING

Weave in loose ends.

BAND AND HANDLE

With Black, cir needle, and RS facing, pick-knit 1 st in the tip of Square 66, 18 sts along the left side of Square 66, 18 sts each along Squares 64, 61, and 60, 1 st in the tip of Square 50, 18 sts each along Squares 59, 69, 71, and 72, 1 st in the tip of Square 72—147 sts for first side of bag band, turn work, and K-CO 145 sts for handle—292 sts total.

Rnd 1: Purl.

Rnd 2: Knit to 1 st before the st in the tip of Square 50, sl 1 kwise, k2tog, psso, knit to end—290 sts.

Rnd 3: Purl.

Rep Rnds 2 and 3 five more times—280 sts;

work 2 more rnds without dec—8 garter ridges on RS.

Add a double-knitted edging as foll: Using the first st of the rnd as a foundation, K-CO 5 new sts—297 sts.

Row 1: (RS) K1, sl 1 pwise with yarn in front (wyf), k1, sl 1 pwise, ***p2tog*** (the last of the 5 new K-CO sts tog with the first st of the edge). Turn work.

Row 2: (WS) Sl 1 pwise wyf, [k1, sl 1 pwise wyf] 2 times.

Rep Rows 1 and 2 until 5 sts rem, ending with a WS row. BO rem 5 sts.

With Black threaded on a tapestry needle, sew the BO and K-CO edges tog as invisibly as possible.

Rep for the other side, beginning at the tip of Square 72 and pick-knit 147 sts along the first band into the CO loops instead of K-CO 145 sts.

FELTING

Felt the piece in the washing machine according to the guidelines on page 137.

LINING

Add a ***lining*** foll the instructions on page 138, matching the shape of the finished bag.

chapter five
knit incomplete squares and blocks

"Incomplete" squares are worked just like regular squares (page 6), but the stitches are bound off after just six garter ridges have been worked. This produces L-shaped motifs, that when joined into blocks, form an unusual openwork pattern.

MAKING AN INCOMPLETE SQUARE

The following instructions are for making two sizes, which is all that is specified for the projects in this book. But, once you understand the principle behind the construction, you can make unfinished squares in any size—simply work as for a regular square but bind off the stitches when the desired number of garter ridges has been worked.

K-CO 25 (31) sts. (The incomplete square in the photograph began with 25 stitches.)

Row 1: (WS) Knit to the last st, p1 (*edge st*). **Note:** The first stitch of subsequent rows will always be slipped, but you need to anchor it by knitting it on Row 1.

Row 2: (RS) Sl 1 kwise (edge st), k10 (13), *sl 1 kwise, k2tog, psso,* k10 (13), p1 (edge st)—2 sts decreased.

Rows 3, 5, 7, and 9: Sl 1 knitwise, knit to the last st, p1.

Row 4: Sl 1 kwise, k9 (12), sl 1 kwise, k2tog, psso, k9 (12), p1—21 (27) sts.

Row 6: Sl 1 kwise, k8 (11), sl 1 kwise, k2tog, psso, k8 (11), p1—19 (25) sts.

Row 8: Sl 1 kwise, k7 (10), sl 1 kwise, k2tog, psso, k7 (10), p1—17 (23) sts.

Row 10: Sl 1 kwise, k6 (9), sl 1 kwise, k2tog, psso, k6 (9), p1—15 (21) sts.

Row 11: Sl 1 kwise, knit to last st, p1—6 garter ridges on RS.

BO all sts knitwise (do not slip the first st) and *at the same time* work a double decrease on the center 3 sts as before—13 (19) sts total BO.

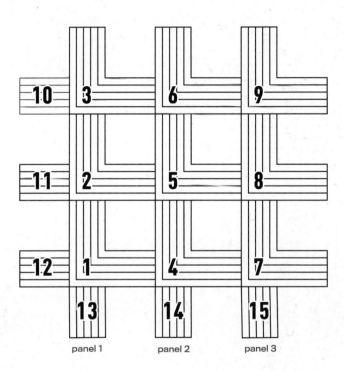

panel 1   panel 2   panel 3

HOW TO JOIN INCOMPLETE
SQUARES INTO A BLOCK

The block shown on page 111 is made up of 3 panels, each made up of 3 incomplete squares. For the first panel, the "squares" are worked one on top of another. The second panel is worked in a series of 3 "squares" (also worked from the bottom up) that are attached to the right edge of "squares" in the first panel as they are knitted. The third panel is worked along the right edge of the second. To give a symmetrical look to the block, knitted "tabs" are added along the two straight sides of the block.

To practice knitting and joining incomplete squares to form a block, gather three colors of sportweight yarn and needles suitable for this yarn weight (sizes 3 to 5 [3.25 to 3.73] mm). In this example, Color 1 is lavender, Color 2 is light blue, and Color 3 is chartreuse. Use the finished block as a decorative hot pad for your table.

PANEL 1

‹ *Incomplete Square 1*
With Color 1, **K-CO** 31 sts.
Row 1: (WS) Knit to the last st, pl (**edge st**).
Row 2: (RS) Sl 1 kwise, k13, **sl 1 kwise, k2tog, psso,** k13, p1—29 sts.

Row 3: Sl1 kwise, knit to the last st, pl.
Row 4: Sl 1 kwise, knit to 1 st before the center st (i.e., k12), sl 1 kwise, k2tog, psso, knit to the last st (i.e., k12), pl—2 sts decreased.
Rep Rows 3 and 4 until 21 sts rem, then rep Row 3 once more 6—garter ridges on RS. **BO** to the last st kwise (do not slip the first st), working a double decrease as before on the center 3 sts—19 sts total BO; 1 st rem (**end st**).

‹ *Incomplete Square 2*
Rotate Square 1 so that the left selvedge edge is at the top and the end st is at the right edge. With Color 2, K-CO 9 new sts (10 sts on left needle), **turn work,** then knit these 10 sts, then **pick-knit** 5 sts along the upper side of the previous square (1 st after each garter ridge), go **"around the corner"** of the left side of the same square and pick-knit 1 st in the nearest CO loop, turn work, and K-CO 15 more sts—31 sts total. Work as for Square 1.

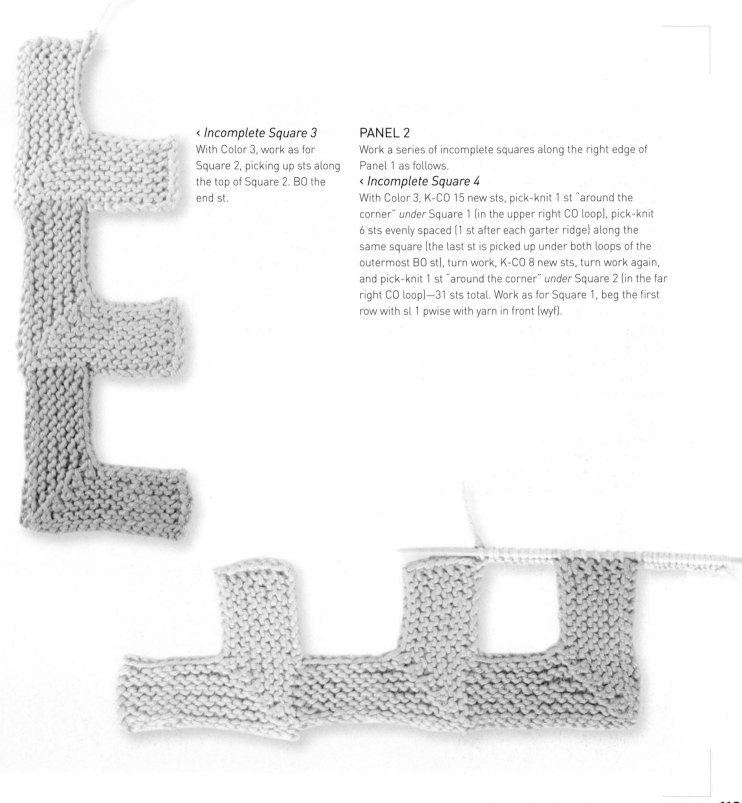

‹ Incomplete Square 3

With Color 3, work as for Square 2, picking up sts along the top of Square 2. BO the end st.

PANEL 2

Work a series of incomplete squares along the right edge of Panel 1 as follows.

‹ Incomplete Square 4

With Color 3, K-CO 15 new sts, pick-knit 1 st "around the corner" *under* Square 1 (in the upper right CO loop), pick-knit 6 sts evenly spaced (1 st after each garter ridge) along the same square (the last st is picked up under both loops of the outermost BO st), turn work, K-CO 8 new sts, turn work again, and pick-knit 1 st "around the corner" *under* Square 2 (in the far right CO loop)—31 sts total. Work as for Square 1, beg the first row with sl 1 pwise with yarn in front (wyf).

‹ Incomplete Square 5

Hold the needle with the end st in your left hand and with Color 1, K-CO 9 more sts—10 sts on needle. Knit these 10 sts, then pick-knit 5 sts evenly spaced (1 st after each garter ridge) along upper edge of Square 4, 1 st in the gap between Squares 4, 1, and 2, and 6 sts evenly spaced along the right edge of Square 2, turn work, K-CO 8 new sts, turn work again, pick-knit 1 st "around the corner" *under* Square 3 in the far right CO loop—31 sts total. Work as for Square 1 but beg the first row with sl 1 pwise wyf.

‹ Incomplete Square 6

With Color 2, work as for Square 5, picking up sts along the upper edge of Square 5 and right edge of Square 3. BO the end st of Square 6.

PANEL 3

Work three squares as for Panel 2, picking up sts along the edge of Squares 4, 5, and 6, and working with Color 2, Color 3, and Color 1, respectively.

‹ Tabs

To make all four edges of the block look the same, you'll need to knit little "tabs" on Squares 1, 2, 3, 4, and 7. To avoid confusion, these tabs continue the numbering sequence of the squares.

‹ Tab 10

Turn the block so that Squares 1, 2, and 3 (Panel 1) are at the top. Beg where Square 2 meets Square 3, count 6 CO loops from left to right along the top of Square 3. With Color 1 and working from right to left, pick-knit 1 st in each of these 6 loops, then turn work and K-CO 8 new sts—14 sts total. Knit the tab while attaching it to the picked-up sts as foll:

Row 1: (WS) K7, sl 1 pwise with yarn in back (wyb), k1, psso, turn work—13 sts.
Row 2: (RS) Sl 1 pwise with yarn in front (wyf), k6, p1.
Row 3: Sl 1 kwise, k6, sl 1, k1, psso, turn work—12 sts.
Row 4: Sl 1 kwise, k6, p1.

Rep Rows 3 and 4 until all the pick-knitted sts have been used and only 8 sts rem, ending with a WS row. With RS facing and slipping the first st pwise wyf, BO all sts—6 garter ridges on RS.

‹ Tab 11

Count 6 CO loops from left to right (where Square 1 meets Square 2) along the top of Square 2. With Color 3, pick-knit 1 st in each of these 6 loops, then K-CO 8 new sts—14 sts total. Work as for Tab 10.

‹ Tab 12

Count 6 CO loops from the left edge of Square 1. With Color 2, pick-knit 1 st in each of these 6 loops, then K-CO 8 new sts—14 sts total. Work as for Tab 10.

‹ *Tab 13*

Turn the block so that Squares 1, 4, and 7 are at the top. With Color 3, pick-knit 1 st in each of the first 6 CO loops at the right edge of Square 1, then turn work and K-CO 8 new sts—14 sts total. Work as for Tab 10.

‹ *Tab 14*

With Color 2, pick-knit 1 st in each of the first 6 CO loops at the right edge of Square 4, then K-CO 8 new sts—14 sts total. Work as for Tab 10.

‹ *Tab 15*

With Color 1, pick-knit 1 st in each of the first 6 CO loops at the right edge of Square 7, then K-CO 8 new sts—14 sts total. Work as for Tab 10.

To make a simple

embellishment for a pillow, work the sample block in a single color of wool yarn, felt it, and attach it to a coordinating pillow with decorative buttons.

pillow with tabs

This pillow cover is a modified sixty-six-square block of incomplete squares that alternate between black and charcoal checkerboard fashion and is accented with two brightly colored "squares." The accent squares are worked in the round on double-pointed needles, beginning at the outer edge and decreasing to the center hole. The entire piece is felted and then sewn onto a colorful pillow so that the tabs extend beyond the pillow edge. The color of the pillow fabric peeks through the holes between the unfinished squares to add spark to the design.

[materials]

FINISHED SIZE Before felting: About 19" by 19" (48 by 48 cm), including tabs. After felting: About 15" by 15" (38 by 38 cm), including tabs.

YARN Fingering weight (#1 Super Fine) in 4 colors.

Shown here: Harrisville New England Knitter's Shetland (100% wool; 217 yd [200 m]/50 g): Black, Charcoal, Poppy, Magenta, 1 skein each.

NEEDLES Size U.S. 4 (3.5): domino needles (page 6) and set of 5 double-pointed (dpn). Adjust needle size if necessary to obtain the correct gauge.

NOTIONS Tapestry needle; 16" (40.5 cm) square fabric-covered pillow (pillow shown is covered with silk); sharp-point sewing needle and matching thread.

GAUGE Each incomplete square measures about 2¼" by 2¼" (5.6 by 5.6 cm) before felting; 1¾" by 1¾" (4.4 by 4.4 cm) after felting.

[techniques]

▼ incomplete squares and blocks (page 110)
▼ reading charts (page 10)
▼ weave in tails as you knit (page 12)
▼ see Glossary (page 133) for abbreviations and highlighted terms

[notes]

▼ Work the incomplete squares and tabs in garter stitch in numerical order and in the colors specified on the chart.
▼ The direction of the numbers on the chart indicates the knitting direction.

PANEL 1

‹ *Incomplete Square 1*

With Black, ***K-CO*** 25 sts.

Row 1: (WS) Knit to the last st, p1 (**edge st**).

Row 2: (RS) Sl 1 kwise (edge st), knit to 1 st before center st (i.e., k10), ***sl 1 kwise, k2tog, psso,*** knit to last st (i.e., k10), p1 (edge st)—23 sts.

Row 3: Sl 1 kwise, knit to the last st, p1.

Row 4: Sl 1 kwise, knit to 1 st before the center st, sl 1 kwise, k2tog, psso, knit to the last st, p1—2 sts decreased.

Rep Rows 3 and 4 until 15 sts rem, then rep Row 3 once more—4 garter ridges on RS.

BO to the last st kwise (do not slip the first st) and *at the same time* work a double decrease on the center 3 sts as before—13 sts total BO; 1 st rem (**end st**) on right needle.

‹ *Incomplete Square 2*

Rotate Square 1 so that the left selvedge edge is at the top and the end st is at the right edge. With Charcoal, K-CO 6 new sts (7 sts on left needle), then knit these 7 sts, then ***pick-knit*** 5 sts along the upper edge of Square 1, go ***"around the corner"*** of the left edge of the same square and pick-knit 1 st in the nearest CO-loop, turn work, and K-CO 12 more sts—25 sts total. Work as for Square 1.

‹ *Incomplete Squares 3 to 8*

Foll the placement and colors specified on the chart, work as for Square 2. ***BO*** the end st of Square 8.

BEGIN PANEL 2

‹ *Incomplete Square 9*

With Charcoal, K-CO 12 sts, pick-knit 1 st "around the corner" *under* the lowest square of the last worked panel (Square 1) in the far right CO loop, 6 sts evenly spaced along the same square (the last st is picked up under both loops of the outermost BO st), turn work, K-CO 5 new sts, turn work again, and pick-knit 1 st "around the corner" *under* Square 2 in the far right CO loop—25 sts total. Work as for Square 1, but beg the first row with sl 1 pwise with yarn in front (wyf).

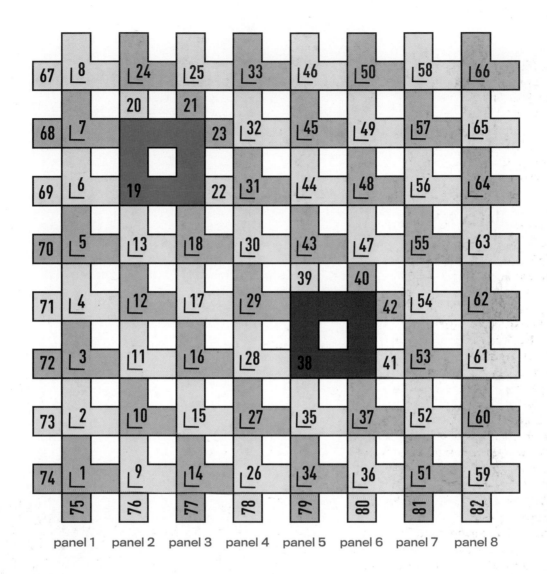

Black
Charcoal
Poppy
Magenta

panel 1 panel 2 panel 3 panel 4 panel 5 panel 6 panel 7 panel 8

‹ *Incomplete Square 10*
Hold the needle in your left hand and with Black, K-CO 6 new sts—7 sts on needle. Knit these 7 sts, then pick-knit 5 sts evenly spaced along upper edge of last worked square (Square 9), 1 st in the gap between Squares 9, 1, and 2, and 6 sts along the right edge of Square 2, turn work, K-CO 5 new sts, turn work again, and pick-knit 1 st "around the corner" *under* the third lowest square of previous panel in the far right CO-loop (Square 3)—25 sts total. Work as for Square 1 but beg the first row with sl 1 pwise wyf.

‹ *Incomplete Squares 11, 12, and 13*
Work as for Square 10, alternating Charcoal and Black. The rest of this panel will be completed later. End Square 13 by pulling the end st loose, cutting the yarn, and threading the tail through it.

BEGIN PANEL 3
‹ *Incomplete Squares 14 to 18*
Foll the placement and colors specified on the chart, work as for Squares 9 to 13 of Panel 2.

REMAINING PART OF PANELS 2 AND 3
‹ *Large Square 19*
With Poppy and double-pointed needles, work 76 sts foll.

Needle 1: Insert needle into end st of Square 13 (pull the end st tail tight to secure this st), K-CO 3 more st—4 sts on needle. Knit these 4 sts, then pick-knit 5 sts along the upper side of Square 13, 1 st in the gap between Squares 13, 5, and 6, and 6 sts along the right edge of Square 6, turn work, and K-CO 3 new sts—19 sts on this needle.

Needle 2: K-CO 2 more sts, turn work, pick-knit 1 st "around the corner" *under* Square 7, then 6 sts along the right edge of Square 7, turn work again, and K-CO 10 new sts—19 sts on this needle.

Needle 3: K-CO 19 new sts—19 sts on this needle.

Needle 4: K-CO 10 new sts, turn work, pick-knit 1 st into the edge st of Square 18, and 5 sts along the upper side of the same square—19 sts on this needle; 76 sts total.

Rnds 1, 3, 5, 7, and 9: Purl.

Rnd 2: *K8, sl 1 kwise, k2tog, psso, k8; rep from * for rem 3 needles—68 sts.

Rnd 4: *K7, sl 1 wise, k2tog, psso, k7; rep from * for rem 3 needles—60 sts.

Rnd 6: *K6, sl 1 kwise, k2tog, psso, k6; rep from * for rem 3 needles—52 sts.

Rnd 8: *K5, sl 1 kwise, k2tog, psso, k5; rep from * for rem 3 needles—44 sts.

Rnd 10: *K4, sl 1 kwise, k2tog, psso, k4; rep from * for rem 3 needles—36 sts.

Rnd 11: Purl.

BO all sts and *at the same time* sl 1 kwise, k2tog, psso in each corner—28 sts total BO.

‹ *Tab 20*
Rotate the piece so Square 19 is at the top. Count 6 CO loops from Square 7 toward the right. With Charcoal, pick-knit 1 st in each of these 6 loops and 1 st in the upper left corner of Square 19, turn work, and K-CO 6 new sts—13 sts total.

Row 1: (WS) K6, sl 1 kwise, k1, psso, turn work.

Row 2: Sl 1 pwise with yarn in front (wyf), k5, p1.

Row 3: Sl 1 kwise, k5, **ssk**. Rep Rows 2 and 3 until all picked up sts have been used, ending with WS Row 3—7 sts. BO while working according to Row 2, but pull the last st loose, cut the yarn, and thread the tail through it.

‹ *Tab 21*
With Black, pick-knit 1 st in the upper right corner of Square 19, then 6 more sts toward Tab 20, turn work, and K-CO 6 more sts—13 sts total. Work as for Tab 20.

‹ *Tab 22*
Rotate piece so Panel 1 is along the bottom and with Black and RS facing, pick-knit 1 st into the upper right corner of Square 19 between Squares 18 and 19, 6 more sts along Square 19 toward Square 21, turn work, and K-CO 6 new sts—13 sts total. Work as for Tab 20. BO the end st.

< *Tab 23*

Count 6 CO loops from the corner between Squares 19 and 21 to the right and with Black, pick-knit 1 st in each of these 6 loops, 1 st in the corner, turn work, and K-CO 6 more sts—13 sts total. Work as for Tab 22.

< *Incomplete Squares 24 and 25*

Foll the placement and colors specified on the chart, work as for Square 10 but beg the Square on top of the tab and knit the last st of the tab (pull the tab-st tail tight to secure this st).

PANEL 4

Foll the placement and colors specified on the chart, work as for Squares 9 to 13 of Panel 2.

PANELS 5 AND 6

Foll the placement and colors specified on the chart, work as for Panels 2 and 3, working large Square 38 as for large Square 19, but with Magenta instead of Poppy; work Tabs 39 and 40 as for Tabs 20 and 21; work Tabs 41 and 42 as for Tabs 22 and 23.

PANELS 7 AND 8

Foll the placement and colors specified on the chart, work as for Panel 4.

TABS

Add tabs to the left and bottom edges as for those on the right and top edges, following the placement and colors specified on the chart.

< *Tab 67*

Rotate the piece so that Squares 8, 7, 6, etc. (Panel 1) are at the top. Count 6 CO loops from left to right (where Square 7 meets Square 8) along the top of Square 8. With

Charcoal, pick-knit 1 st in each of these 6 loops, turn work, and K-CO 6 new sts—13 sts total. Work as for Tab 20. BO the end st.

< *Tabs 68 to 74*

Foll the placement and colors specified on the chart, work as for Tab 67.

< *Tab 75*

Rotate the piece so that Squares 1, 9, 14, etc., are at the top. With Black, pick-knit 1 st in the right corner of Square 1, then 6 more sts along the edge of the same square, turn work, and K-CO 6 new sts—13 sts total. Work as for Tab 20. BO the end st.

< *Tabs 76 to 82*

Foll the placement and colors specified on the chart, work as for Tab 75.

FINISHING

Weave in loose ends. Felt the piece in the washing machine according to the guidelines on page 137. Remove it from the machine, lay it on a towel on a flat surface, and stretch and shape the tabs, making sure to maintain the square shape. Allow to air-dry thoroughly. If necessary, you may have to stretch it while steam-ironing it.

With sharp-point sewing needle and matching thread, sew the felted piece onto a pillow so that the tabs extend beyond the edges of the pillow.

abstract stole

This stunning stole shows what fun you can have knitting panels of incomplete squares. I knitted nine panels of twenty-nine incomplete squares in a zigzag pattern of five colors of wool. Panel 9 includes both incomplete squares that form tabs that extend to the right edge and narrow bands that maintain a straight edge. This gives an interesting asymmetrical edge that is mirrored along the left edge of Panel 1 with small tabs knitted onto some of the incomplete squares. Additional tabs and bands are added to each of the short ends of the stole. To finish, the piece is felted in the washing machine. Adjust the size by adding or subtracting the number of squares in each panel or by working more or fewer panels.

[materials]

FINISHED SIZE Before felting: About 26" (66 cm) wide and 80" (204 cm) long, including tabs. After felting: About 22½" (57 cm) wide and 69½" (177 cm) long, including tabs.

YARN Fingering weight (#1 Super Fine) in 5 colors.

Shown here: Harrisville New England Knitter's Shetland (100% wool; 217 yd [200 m]/50 g): Foliage (gold), Poppy (orange), 3 skeins each; Grass (green), Pink, 2 skeins each; Magenta, 1 skein.

NEEDLES Size U.S. 4 (3.5 mm): domino needles (page 6). Adjust needle size if necessary to obtain the correct gauge.

NOTIONS Tapestry needle.

GAUGE Each incomplete square measures about 2¾" by 2¾" (6.9 by 6.9 cm) before felting; about 2½" by 2½" (6 by 6 cm) after felting.

[techniques]

▸ incomplete squares and blocks (page 110)
▸ reading charts (page 10)
▸ weave in tails as you knit (page 12)
▸ see Glossary (page 133) for abbreviations and highlighted terms

[notes]

▸ Work the incomplete squares, bands, and tabs in garter stitch in numerical order and in the colors specified on the chart.
▸ The direction of the numbers on the chart indicates the knitting direction.

PANEL 1

‹ *Incomplete Square 1*

With Grass, **K-CO** 31 sts.

Row 1: (WS) Knit to the last st, p1 (**edge st**).

Row 2: (RS) Sl 1 kwise (edge st), knit to 1 st before the center st (i.e., k13), **sl 1 kwise, k2tog, psso,** knit to the last st (i.e., k13), p1 (edge st)—29 sts.

Row 3: Sl 1 kwise, knit to the last st, p1.

Row 4: Sl 1 kwise, knit to 1 st before the center st, sl 1 kwise, k2tog, psso, knit to the last st, p1—27 sts.

Rep Rows 3 and 4 until 21 sts rem, then rep Row 3 once more—6 garter ridges on RS. **BO** to the last st kwise (do not slip the first st), working a double decrease as before on the center 3 sts—19 sts total BO; 1 st rem on right needle (**end st**).

‹ *Incomplete Square 2*

Rotate Square 1 so that the left selvedge edge is at the top and the end st is at the right edge. With Poppy, K-CO 9 new sts (10 sts on right needle), then knit these 10 sts, then **pick-knit** 5 sts along the upper side of Square 1 (1 st after each garter ridge), go **"around the corner"** of the left side of the same square and pick-knit 1 st in the nearest CO loop, **turn work,** and K-CO 15 more sts—31 sts total. Work as for Square 1 but sl the first st pwise wyf.

‹ *Incomplete Squares 3 to 28*

Foll the placement and colors specified on the chart, work as for Square 2.

‹ *Incomplete Square 29*

With Poppy, work as for Square 28. BO the end st.

PANEL 2

‹ *Incomplete Square 30*

With Grass, K-CO 15 new sts, pick-knit 1 st "around the corner" *under* Square 1 in the far right CO loop, 6 sts (1 st after each garter ridges) along the same square (the last st is picked up under both loops of the outermost BO st), turn work, K-CO 8 new sts, turn work again, and pick-knit 1 st "around the corner" *under* Square 2 in the far right CO loop—31 sts total. Work as for Square 1 but beg the first row with sl 1 pwise with yarn in front (wyf).

‹ *Incomplete Square 31*

Hold the needle with the end st in your left hand and with Green, K-CO 9 more sts—10 sts on needle. Knit these 10 sts, then pick-knit 5 sts evenly spaced along upper edge of Square 4, 1 st in the hole between Squares 2, 1, and 30, and 6 sts along the right edge of Square 2, turn work, K-CO 8 new sts, turn work again, then pick-knit 1 st "around the corner" *under* Square 3 in the far right CO loop—31 sts total. Work as for Square 1 but beg the first row with sl 1 pwise wyf.

‹ *Incomplete Squares 32 to 57*

Foll the placement and colors specified on the chart, work as for Square 31.

‹ *Incomplete Square 58*

With Poppy, work as for Square 29 but K-CO 9 sts instead of 8 (as it is not possible to pick-knit "around the corner" *under* the square here). BO the end st.

PANELS 3 AND 4

Foll the placement and colors specified on the chart, work as for Panel 2.

PANEL 5

‹ *Incomplete Squares 117 to 144*

Foll the placement and colors specified on the chart, work as for Squares 30 to 57 of Panel 2.

‹ *Horizontal Band 145*

Hold the needle with the end st in your left hand with the needle pointing to the right and K-CO 9 new sts (10 sts on needle), knit

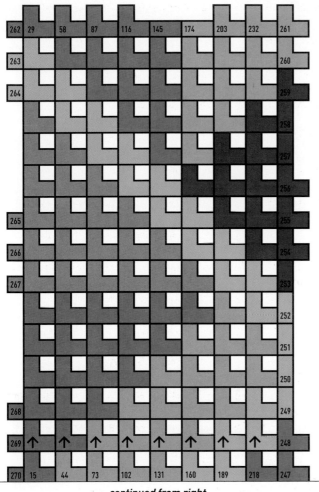

262	29	58	87	116	145	174	203	232	261
263									260
264									259
									258
									257
									256
									255
265									254
266									253
267									252
									251
									250
268									249
269	↑	↑	↑	↑	↑	↑	↑	↑	248
270	15	44	73	102	131	160	189	218	247

continued from right

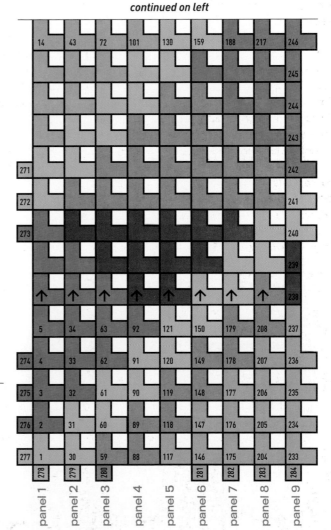

continued on left

	14	43	72	101	130	159	188	217	246
									245
									244
									243
271									242
272									241
273									240
									239
	↑	↑	↑	↑	↑	↑	↑	↑	238
	5	34	63	92	121	150	179	208	237
274	4	33	62	91	120	149	178	207	236
275	3	32	61	90	119	148	177	206	235
276	2	31	60	89	118	147	176	205	234
277	1	30	59	88	117	146	175	204	233
278	279	280			281	282	283	284	

panel 1   panel 2   panel 3   panel 4   panel 5   panel 6   panel 7   panel 8   panel 9

 Foliage
Poppy
Pink
Magenta
Grass

these 10 sts, then pick-knit 5 sts along the upper edge of Square 144, 1 st in the gap between Squares 144, 115, and 116, and 6 sts along the left edge of Square 116—22 sts total.

Row 1: (WS) Knit to the last st, p1 (edge st).
Row 2: (RS) Sl 1 kwise, k13, sl 1 kwise, k2tog, psso, k4, p1—20 sts.
Rows 3, 5, 7, and 9: Sl 1 kwise, knit to the last st, p1.
Row 4: Sl 1 kwise, k12, sl 1 kwise, k2tog, psso, k3, p1—18 sts.
Row 6: Sl 1 kwise, k11, sl 1 kwise, k2tog, psso, k2, p1—16 sts.
Row 8: Sl 1 kwise, k10, sl 1 kwise, k2tog, psso, k1, p1—14 sts.
Row 10: Sl 1 kwise, k9, sl 1 kwise, k2tog, psso, p1—12 sts.
Row 11: Sl 1 kwise, knit to the last st, p1.
Row 12: BO all sts and *at the same time* work the last 3 sts as sl 1 kwise, k2tog, psso. BO end st.

PANEL 6
Foll the placement and colors specified on the chart, work as for Panel 5.

PANELS 7 AND 8
Foll the placement and colors specified on the chart, work as for Panel 2.

PANEL 9
‹ *Incomplete Squares 233 to 236*
Foll the placement and colors specified on the chart, work as for Squares 30 to 33 of Panel 2.
‹ *Vertical Band 237*
Hold the needle with the end st from Square 236 in your right hand and pick-knit 5 sts along the upper side of Square 236 (6 sts on right needle), 1 st in the gap between

Squares 236, 207, and 208, 6 sts along Square 208, turn work, K-CO 8 more sts, turn work again, and pick-knit 1 st "around the corner" *under* Square 209—22 sts total.

Row 1: (WS) Sl 1 pwise wyf, knit to the last st, p1 (edge st).

Row 2: (RS) Sl 1 kwise, k4, sl 1 kwise, k2tog, psso, knit to the last st, p1—20 sts.

Rows 3, 5, 7, and 9: Sl 1 kwise, knit to the last st, p1.

Row 4: Sl 1 kwise, k3, sl 1 kwise, k2tog, psso, knit to the last st, p1—18 sts.

Row 6: Sl 1 kwise, k2, sl 1 kwise, k2tog, psso, knit to the last st, p1—16 sts.

Row 8: Sl 1 kwise, k1, sl 1 kwise, k2tog, psso, knit to the last st, p1—14 sts.

Row 10: Sl 1 kwise, sl 1 kwise, k2tog, pass the last slipped st over the k2tog st, knit to the last st, p1—12 sts.

Row 11: Sl 1 kwise, knit to the last st, p1.

Row 12: Sl 1 kwise, k2tog, psso, BO 9 sts—1 st rem (end st).

‹ *Vertical Bands 238 and 239*

Foll the placement and colors specified on the chart, work as for Vertical Band 237.

‹ *Incomplete Squares and Vertical Bands 240 to 260*

Following the placement and colors specified on the chart, work squares as for Square 233 and vertical bands as for Vertical Band 237.

‹ *Incomplete Square 261*

With Foliage, work as for Square 29.

TABS

Add tabs to the left and bottom edges as for those on the right and top edges, foll the colors and placement specified on the chart as foll.

‹ *Tab 262*

Rotate the piece so that Squares 1 to 29 (Panel 1) are at the top. Count 6 CO loops from left to right (where Square 28 meets Square 29) along the edge of Square 29. With Poppy, pick-knit 1 st in each of these 6 loops, turn work, and K-CO 8 new sts—14 sts total. Knit the tab while attaching it to the picked-up sts as foll:

Row 1: (WS) K7, sl 1 pwise with yarn in back (wyb), k1, psso, turn work—13 sts.

Row 2: (RS) Sl 1 pwise with yarn in front (wyf), k6, p1.

Row 3: Sl 1 kwise, k6, sl 1 pwise wyb, k1, psso, turn work—12 sts.

Row 4: Sl 1 kwise, k6, p1.

Rep Rows 3 and 4 until all the pick-knitted sts have been used and only 8 sts rem. With WS facing and slipping the first st pwise wyf, BO all sts—6 garter ridges on RS.

‹ *Tabs 263 to 277*

Foll the placement and colors specified on the chart, work as for Tab 262.

‹ *Tab 278*

Rotate the piece so that the bottom edge (Squares 233, 204, etc.) is at the top. With Grass and beg at the right corner of Square 1, pick-knit 6 sts towards Square 30, turn work, and K-CO 8 new sts—14 sts total. Work as for Tab 262.

‹ *Tabs 279 to 284*

Foll the placement and colors specified on the chart, work as for Tab 278.

FINISHING

Weave in loose ends. Felt the stole in the washing machine according to the guidelines on page 137. Remove it from the machine, lay it on a towel on a flat surface, and stretch and shape the tabs, making sure that the two long edges are the same length. Allow to air-dry thoroughly.

bobble scarf

This unusual scarf is constructed much the same as the Candy Stole on page 16 but with incomplete squares that are worked in panels that grow along the diagonal. To give straight edges to the scarf, each panel begins and/or ends with a solid triangle. Colorful seven-stitch bobbles punctuate the third row of each incomplete square, and a solid band closes the gaps between the incomplete squares of the last three panels. The bobbles on this band are worked separately and sewn in place. To finish, the scarf is machine-felted. The squares worked here are bound off when the stitches have been decreased from 31 to 25 stitches. If you'd like smaller holes, work a few more rows in each square and bind off the stitches when 19, 17, or 15 stitches remain and adjust the row that the bobbles are worked on accordingly.

[materials]

FINISHED SIZE Before felting: About 11½" (29.5 cm) wide and 92½" (235 cm) long from tip to tip. After felting: About 9¼" (23.5 cm) wide and 73½" (187 cm) long from tip to tip.
YARN Fingering weight (#1 Super Fine) in 4 colors.
Shown here: Harrisville New England Knitter's Shetland (100% wool; 217 yd [200 m]/50 g): Blackberry (purple; MC), 5 skeins; Lady Slipper (pink; CC1), Melon (orange; CC2), Gold (CC3), 1 skein each.
NEEDLES Size U.S. 4 (3.5) domino needles (page 6) and set of 2 double-pointed (dpn). Adjust needle size if necessary to obtain the correct gauge.
NOTIONS Tapestry needle; size U.S. C/2 (2.75 mm) crochet hook.
GAUGE Each square measures about 2¾" by 2¾" (6.9 by 6.9 cm) wide and about 3¾" (9.8 cm) along the diagonal before felting; about 2¼" by 2¼" (5.5 by 5.5 cm) wide and about 3" (7.8 cm) along the diagonal after felting.

[techniques]

▼ incomplete squares and blocks (page 110)
▼ reading charts (page 10)
▼ weave in tails as you knit (page 12)
▼ see Glossary (page 133) for abbreviations and highlighted terms

[notes]

▼ The chart shows the beginning of the scarf (6 diagonal panels) and the end of the scarf (4 diagonal panels), but not the center 14 panels (Panels 7 to 20). These Panels are worked as for Panel 4.
▼ Work the squares and triangles in garter stitch in numerical order.
▼ The direction of the numbers on the chart indicates the knitting direction.
▼ Refer to the chart for the colors to work the bobbles.

PANEL 1

‹ Incomplete Square 1

With MC, **K-CO** 31 sts.

Row 1: (WS) Knit to last st, p1 (**edge st**).

Row 2: (RS) Sl 1 kwise, knit to 1 st before center st (i.e., k13), **sl 1 kwise, k2tog, psso,** knit to last st (i.e., k13), p1—29 sts.

Row 3: (WS; bobble row) Sl 1 kwise, k13, with Melon, then make a bobble as foll·

bring MC in front (to the WS), join CC and ([k1, yo] 3 times, k1) all in the same st, *bring CC to front between the 2 needles, slip these 7 sts onto the left needle, and k7; rep from * 3 more times, bring CC to the front again and slip these 7 sts onto the left needle, and **k2tog, k3tog,** k2tog, then pass the 2nd and 3rd st over the first. Pull the last CC st loose, cut the yarn, and thread the tail through the st, leaving the bobble on the RS until later. Bring MC in position to knit again, k13, p1. (Bobble will be secured to the square on Row 8.)

Row 4: Sl 1 kwise, k12, k2tog, k12, p1—27 sts.

Rows 5 and 7: Sl 1 kwise, knit to last st, p1.

Row 6: Sl 1 kwise, k11, sl 1 kwise, k2tog, psso, k11, p1—25 sts.

Row 8: Sl 1 kwise, k10, sl 1 kwise, place the last bobble st on the right needle (bring the CC yarn tails to the WS), k2tog, pass both the CC and MC st over the k2tog st, pull the CC tails tight, k10, p1—25 sts.

Row 9: Sl 1 kwise, knit to last st, p1.

BO (do not sl the first st) to the last st knit-wise and *at the same time* work a double decrease on the center 3 sts as before—1 st rem (**end st**).

‹ Incomplete Square 2

Hold the needle with the end st in the left hand and K-CO 10 new sts (11 sts on needle). Knit these 11 sts, then **pick-knit** 4 sts along the left edge of Square 1, go **"around the corner"** of the same square and pick-knit 1 st in the nearest CO loop, turn work, and K-CO 15 more sts—31 sts total. Work as for Square 1 but sl the first st pwise wyf.

‹ Incomplete Square 3

Foll the placement and color specified on the chart, work as for Square 2.

‹ Triangle 4

Hold the needle with Square 3 and the end st in your left hand and K-CO 10 new sts (11 sts on needle). Knit these 11 sts, pick-knit 4 sts along the left edge of Square 3, go "around the corner" of Square 3 and pick-knit 1 st in the nearest CO loop—16 sts total. **Note:** For future Left Triangles, pick-knit this last st working into the upper edge st of the triangle below and into one loop only instead of both stitch loops.

Row 1: (WS) Sl 1 kwise, k14, p1.

Row 2: (RS) Sl 1 kwise, k12, k2tog, p1—15 sts.

Row 3 and all foll WS-rows to Row 27: Sl 1 kwise, knit to last st, p1.

Row 4 and all foll RS rows to Row 26: Sl 1 kwise, knit to last 3 sts, k2tog, p1—3 sts after Row 26.

Row 28: Sl 1 kwise, k2tog—2 sts.

Row 29: (WS) Sl 1 kwise, p1.

Row 30: K2tog—1 st rem (end st). Pull the end st loose, cut the yarn, and thread the tail through it.

PANEL 2

‹ Incomplete Square 5

K-CO 15 sts, turn work, go "around the corner" *under* Square 1 and pick-knit 1 st in the far right CO loop, pick-knit 5 st along the right side of the same square (picking up the last st under both loops of the last BO st), turn work, K-CO 9 new sts, turn work again, go "around the corner" *under* Square 2 and pick-knit 1 st—31 sts total. Work as for Square 1. **Note:** There will be a notch between Squares 5, 1, and 2.

‹ Incomplete Square 6

Hold the needle with the end st in your left hand and K-CO 10 new sts (11 sts on needle). Knit these 11 sts, pick-knit 10 sts in the V formed by the notch as foll: 4 sts along the right edge of the V, 1 st in the hole, and 5 sts along the left edge of the V, turn work, K-CO 9 sts, turn work again, go "around the corner" *under* the next square (here Square 3), and pick-knit 1 st in the far right CO loop—31 sts total. Work as for Square 1 but beg the first row with sl 1 pwise wyf.

‹ *Incomplete Square 7*

Foll the color and placement specified on the chart, work as for Square 6.

‹ *Incomplete Square 8*

Hold the needle with the end st in your left hand and K-CO 10 new sts (11 sts on needle). Knit these 11 sts, then pick-knit in the V as foll: 4 sts along the right edge of the V, 1 st in the hole, and 15 sts along the left side of the V along Triangle 4, but do not pick-knit the last st into the end st of the triangle below; instead work into the loop right before the end st—31 sts total. Work as for Square 6.

‹ *Triangle 9*

Foll the placement specified on the chart, work as for Triangle 4 but pick-knit 1 loop of the last st in the edge st of the triangle below (here Triangle 4).

PANEL 3

‹ *Incomplete Square 10*

Foll the placement and color specified on the chart, work as for Square 5.

‹ *Incomplete Squares 11, 12, and 13*

Foll the placement and colors specified on the chart, work as for Square 6.

‹ *Incomplete Square 14*

Foll the placement and color specified on the chart, work as for Square 8.

‹ *Triangle 15*

Foll the placement specified on the chart, work as for Triangle 9.

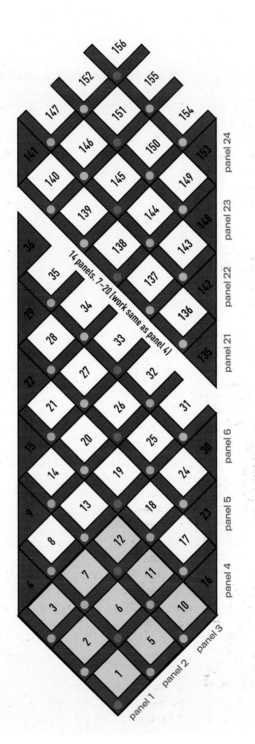

- ● CC1 Lady Slipper
- ● CC2 Melon
- ● CC3 Gold
- ■ MC Blackberry

PANEL 4

‹ Triangle 16

Go "around the corner" *under* Square 10 in the far right CO loop and pick-knit 1 st, then pick-knit 4 sts along the right edge of the square to the left (here Square 10), 1 st under the nearest BO st, turn work, K-CO 9 new sts, turn work again, and pick-knit 1 st "around the corner" *under* the left square (here Square 11) from the previous panel—16 sts total.

Row 1: (WS) Sl 1 kwise, k14, p1.

Row 2: (RS) Sl 1 kwise, sl 1 kwise once more, k1, psso, k12, p1—15 sts.

Row 3 and all WS rows to Row 27: Sl 1 kwise, knit to the last st, p1.

Row 4 and all RS rows to Row 26: Sl 1 kwise, sl 1 more st kwise, k1, psso, knit to last st, p1—1 st decreased each row; 3 sts after Row 26.

Row 28: Sl 1 kwise, p2tog—2 sts.

Row 29: Sl 1 kwise, p1.

Row 30: Sl 1 kwise, k1, psso—1 st rem (end st). Pull the end st loose, cut the yarn, and thread the tail through it.

‹ Incomplete Square 17

Beg right after the end st from Triangle 16, pick-knit 15 sts along the left edge this triangle, 1 st in the hole, 4 sts along the next square, 1 st in the outermost BO st (21 sts on needle), turn work, K-CO 9 new sts, turn work again, and pick-knit 1 st "around the corner" *under* the next square—31 sts total. Work as for Square 6.

‹ Incomplete Squares 18, 19, and 20

Foll the placement and colors specified on the chart, work as for Square 6.

‹ Incomplete Square 21

Foll the placement and colors specified on the chart, work as for Square 8.

‹ Triangle 22

Foll the placement and colors specified on the chart, work as for Triangle 9.

PANELS 5 TO 21

Foll the placement and colors specified on the chart, work as for Panel 4.

PANELS 22, 23, AND 24

Foll the placement and colors specified on the chart, work as for Panel 4 but work 1, 2, and 3 fewer incomplete squares, respectively, per panel.

ENDING

With MC, pick-knit the first st in the end st from Triangle 153 and 5 sts along Square 154, turn work, K-CO 9 new sts, turn work again, pick-knit 1 st "around the corner" *under* Square 155, 5 sts along the same square, turn work again, K-CO 9 new sts, turn work again, pick-knit 1 st "around the corner" *under* the right edge of Square 156, 5 sts along the same square, turn work again, K-CO 10 sts + 1 st (this will be the top st) + 10 more sts, turn work again, pick-knit 5 sts along the left edge of Square 156, go "around the corner" of the same square, pick-knit 1 st in the outermost CO-loop, turn work again, K-CO 9 new sts, turn work again, pick-knit 5 sts along the left edge of Square 152, 1 st "around the corner" of the same square, turn work again, K-CO 9 new sts, turn work again, pick-knit 5 sts along the left edge of Square 147, and 1 st in the edge-st of Triangle 141—93 sts total.

Row 1: (WS) Sl 1 kwise, knit to the last st, p1.

Row 2: (RS) Sl 1 kwise, sl 1 more st kwise, k1, psso, knit to the top-st, *k1f&b* in the top st and k1f&b into the next st, knit to the last 3 sts, k2tog, p1.

Rep Rows 1 and 2 until 9 rows have been worked and there are 6 ridges on the RS. Loosely BO all sts.

FINISHING

Weave in loose ends.

BOBBLES (make 5; 1 in CC2, 2 in CC1, and 2 in CC2)

With dpn and CC specified, loosely CO 1 st.

Row 1: (RS) Work ([k1, yo] 3 times, k1) all in the same st—7 sts.

Row 2: (RS) Push the sts to the opposite end needle (without turning the work) and knit these 7 sts.

Rows 3, 4, and 5: Work as for Row 2.

Row 6: K2tog, k3tog, k2tog, then pass the 2nd and 3rd sts over the first st—1 st rem. BO the last st. Cut yarn leaving a 6" (15 cm) tail. With crochet hook, fasten bobbles to the ending as indicated on chart by pulling the tails to the WS and knotting them together tightly.

Felt in the washing machine according to the guidelines on page 137. Remove it from the machine, lay it on a towel on a flat surface, and stretch and shape the the edges so that the two long edges are the same length. Pinch the bobbles so they stand out above the background.

glossary

beg	begin(s); beginning
BO	bind off
CC	contrast color
cir	circular
cm	centimeter(s)
CO	cast on
cont	continue(s); continuing
dec(s)	decrease(s); decreasing
dpn	double-pointed needle(s)
foll	follow(s); following
g	gram(s)
inc	increase(s); increasing
k	knit
k1f&b	knit into the front and back of the same stitch
K-CO	knitted cast-on
kwise	knitwise; as if to knit (insert needle into stitch from left to right).
MC	main color
mm	millimeter(s)
oz	ounce(s)
p	purl
p1f&b	purl into the front and back of the same stitch
patt(s)	pattern(s)
pick-knit	pick up and knit
psso	pass slipped stitch over
pwise	purlwise, as if to purl (insert needle into stitch from right to left)

rem	remain(s); remaining
rep	repeat(s); repeating
ridge	bumps made on wrong side of a row of knitting; 1 ridge is formed every 2 rows of garter stitch
rnd(s)	round(s)
RS	right side
sl	slip
sl st	slip stitch (slip 1 stitch purlwise unless otherwise indicated)
ssk	slip 2 stitches individually knitwise, return them to the left needle, then knit them together through their back loops.
st(s)	stitch(es)
St st	stockinette stitch
tbl	through back loop (insert right needle through the back leg of the stitch on the left needle)
tog	together
WS	wrong side
wyb	with yarn in back
wyf	with yarn in front
yd	yard(s)
yo	yarnover
*	repeat starting point
( )	alternate measurements and/or instructions
[ ]	work instructions as a group a specified number of times

"AROUND THE CORNER" ▶

To make the edges neat and straight between squares, when picking up and knitting stitches along a previously knitted square, bring the needle tip "around the corner" of the square, picking up and knitting a stitch into a single loop of the edge cast-on stitch.

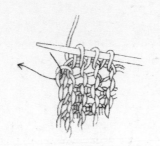

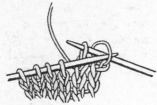

[figure 1]

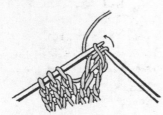

[figure 2]

[figure 3]

BIND-OFFS (BO)
◀ STANDARD BO

Knit the first stitch, *knit the next stitch (two stitches on right needle), insert left needle tip into first stitch on right needle [figure 1] and lift this stitch up and over the second stitch [figure 2] and off the needle [figure 3]. Repeat from * for the desired number of stitches.

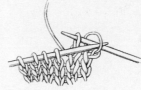

[figure 1]

[figure 2]

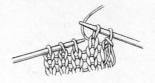

[figure 3]

◀ SUSPENDED BO

For a looser bind-off, slip one stitch, knit one stitch, *insert left needle tip into first stitch on right needle and lift the first stitch over the second, keeping the lifted stitch at the end of the left needle [figure 1]. Skipping the lifted stitch, knit the next stitch [figure 2], then slip both stitches off the left needle—two stitches remain on right needle and one stitch has been bound off [figure 3]. Repeat from * until no stitches remain on left needle, then pass first stitch on right needle over second and off the needle as for the standard BO.

CAST-ONS (CO)
KNITTED CO (K-CO) ▶

Make a slipknot of working yarn and place it on the left needle if there are no stitches already there. *Use the right needle to knit the first stitch (or slipknot) on left needle [figure 1] and place new loop onto left needle in a twisted orientation to form a new stitch [figure 2]. Repeat from * for the desired number of stitches, always working into the last stitch made.

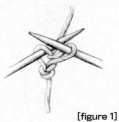

[figure 1]

[figure 2]

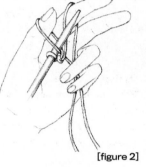

[figure 1]

[figure 2]

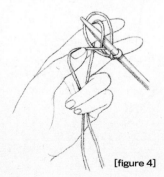

[figure 3]

[figure 4]

◀ LONG-TAIL (CONTINENTAL) CO

Use this method when no type of cast-on is specified. Leaving a long tail (about ½" [1.3 cm] for each stitch to be cast on), make a slipknot and place on right needle. Place thumb and index finger of your left hand between the yarn ends so that working yarn is around your index finger and tail end is around your thumb and secure the yarn ends with your other fingers. Hold your palm upwards, making a V of yarn [figure 1]. *Bring needle up through loop on thumb [figure 2], catch first strand around index finger, and go back down through loop on thumb [figure 3]. Drop loop off thumb and, placing thumb back in V configuration, tighten resulting stitch on needle [figure 4]. Repeat from * for desired number of stitches.

CROCHET
CHAIN (CH) ▶

Make a slipknot and place it on crochet hook if there isn't a loop already on the hook. *Yarn over hook and draw through loop on hook. Repeat from * for the desired number of stitches. To fasten off, cut yarn and draw end through last loop formed.

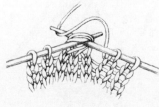

◀ SLIP STITCH

* Insert hook into stitch, yarn over hook and draw a loop through both the stitch and the loop already on the hook. Repeat from *.

DECREASES
◀ K2TOG

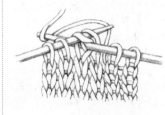

Insert the right needle tip into two stitches at the same time knitwise and knit them together as if they were a single stitch.

◀ K2TOG TBL

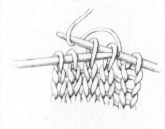

Insert the right needle tip into the back loop of the next two stitches and knit them together as if they were a single stitch.

◀ K3TOG

Work as for k2tog but work three stitches together.

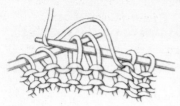

◄ P2TOG
Insert the right-hand needle into two stitches at the same time purlwise and purl them together as if they were a single stitch.

▲ P3TOG Work as for p2tog, but work three stitches together.

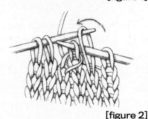

[figure 1]

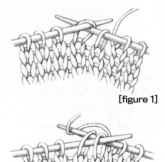

[figure 2]

◄ SL 1 KWISE, K2TOG, PSSO
Slip one stitch knitwise onto right needle, knit the next two stitches together **[figure 1]**, then use the tip of the left needle to lift the slipped stitch up and over the knitted stitches **[figure 2]** and off the needle.

SL 1 KWISE, K1, PSSO ►
Slip one stitch knitwise onto right needle, knit the next stitch **[figure 1]**, then use the tip of the left needle to lift the slipped stitch up and over the knitted stitch and off the needle **[figure 2]**.

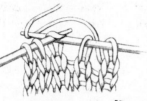

[figure 1]

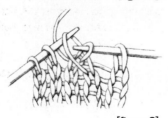

[figure 2]

SSK ►
Slip two stitches individually knitwise **[figure 1]**, insert left needle tip into the front of these two slipped stitches, and use the right needle to knit them together through their back loops **[figure 2]**.

[figure 1]

[figure 2]

EDGE STITCHES

Because domino squares build one on top of another as stitches are picked up and knitted along the edges of one square to form the foundation for the next square, it's important the edge stitches are neat and orderly. To accomplish this, slip the first stitch knitwise of every row (unless otherwise instructed) and always purl the last stitch of every row. It's not uncommon for the edge stitch at the beginning of wrong-side rows to be looser than the others. To compensate, be sure to pull the working yarn snuggly when working the second stitch of these rows. If you're working a striped pattern, you may find that the edge stitch on the right-hand side tends to be too tight. To compensate, stretch the work downward when you slip the first stitch and knit the next one. If that doesn't take care of the problem, before you begin the row, pull the edge stitch below in the stripe that's the same color that you're about to use to help loosen the yarn carried along the edge and allow the edge stitches to relax as more yarn is fed along the edge. The yarn tension and edge stitches should be sufficiently relaxed to maintain a smooth edge of even length and match the other edge. If your work is still too tight, slip the first stitch, yarnover, and work to the end of the row, then drop the yarnover when you come to it on the following row.

TWISTED SELVEDGE ▶

When working a striped pattern that involves color changes every other row, be sure to twist the old and new colors around each other at the color changes, bringing the new color to be used over the top of the color just used **[figure 1]** while paying attention to keeping the same amount of tension on each side of the piece. This will produce a three-legged stitch at the beginning of the color-change rows (two legs of the slipped stitch plus the strand of yarn from the color change). When picking up and knitting along this edge, pick up under all three legs **[figure 2]**.

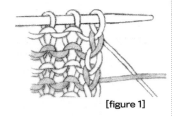

[figure 1]

[figure 2]

END STITCH

The end stitch is the stitch remaining when the final decrease has been made when working a square. If stitches will be picked up for another square on top of the one just finished, the end stitch is considered the first stitch of the new square. Do not worry if the end stitch is a different color than the new square—it won't be apparent in the finished piece. If the end stitch is not going to be used again, secure it by cutting the yarn and pulling the tail through this stitch.

FELTING

Most projects knitted with wool yarn (except superwash wool) will felt into a dense fabric when run through a cycle (or two or three) in the washing machine. The amount of felting depends on the density of the load, water temperature, and agitation so don't be surprised if you get slightly different results than reported here. I like to felt 10 to 18 ounces at a time in lukewarm water along with a couple of tennis balls to increase agitation. To prevent your projects from overfelting, check the progress every few minutes and stop the machine when the desired thickness is achieved. To remove excess water, set the machine on the spin cycle. It is important to get rid of as much water as possible as quickly as possible.

After the pieces have felted to the desired thickness, remove them from the machine and stretch them as needed to achieve the desired shape, then let them air-dry thoroughly. Later, if you'd like to felt a piece a bit more, go over the wrong side with a hot steam iron. You can also encourage the edges to felt more firmly by ironing them, alternating between dry and steam settings.

I-CORD (also called Knit-Cord) ▶

Using two double-pointed needles, cast on the desired number of stitches (usually three to five). *Without turning the needle, slide the stitches to other end of needle, pull the yarn around the back, and knit the stitches again as usual. Repeat from * for the desired length.

INCREASES

K1F&B ▶

Knit into a stitch but leave it on the left needle [figure 1], then knit through the back loop of the same stitch [figure 2] and slip the original stitch off the needle [figure 3].

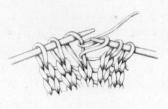

[figure 1]

[figure 2]

[figure 3]

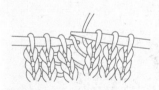

[figure 1]

◀ RAISED MAKE-ONE

With left needle tip, lift the strand between the last knitted stitch and the first stitch on the left needle from front to back [figure 1], then knit the lifted loop through the back [figure 2].

[figure 2]

LINING ▶

Many of the bags in this book are finished off with a lining made of commercial fabric. To line a project, use the felted piece(s) as a template to cut out the lining fabric, allowing for ½" (1.3 cm) seam allowance on all sides. Keep in mind that the felted fabric may stretch a little with use, so it's always a good idea to make the lining slightly bigger. Using a sewing machine, sew the lining pieces together to form the same shape as the felted bag. Fold the seam allowance of the lining upper edge to the wrong side and lightly press in place. With wrong sides facing together, place the lining inside the felted bag and sew the upper edge of the lining to the upper edge of the felted bag. If you want to give the lining more flexibility, cut the lining fabric on the diagonal. For projects made up of three blocks, cut the lining in three sections—one for each block—and sew them together into the pouch shape. For projects made up of four blocks, use the dimensions of the completed bag to cut the lining out of single piece, sew it together, and make gussets to fit the square shape of the bag bottom by sewing across the corners of the lining and folding them up or down as shown. Feel free to cut extra pieces of lining fabric to make pockets.

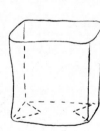

SEAMS
◀ MATTRESS STITCH

Place the pieces to be seamed next to each other with right sides facing up. Begin at the right edge and work toward the left as follows: Insert threaded needle under one bar between the two edge stitches on one piece [figure 1], then under the corresponding bar plus the bar above it on the other piece [figure 2]. *Pick up the next two bars on the first piece [figure 3], then the next two bars on the other. Repeat from *, ending by picking up the last bar or pair of bars on the first piece.

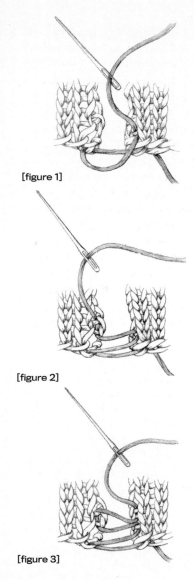

[figure 1]

[figure 2]

[figure 3]

PICK-KNIT ▼
(also called **Pick Up and Knit**)

With the right side of the piece facing, work from right to left according to the type of edge you're working on as follows: Along a selvedge edge: insert the needle tip under both loops of the selvedge stitch, wrap the yarn around the needle [figure 1] and pull a loop through. Along a cast-on edge: insert the needle under just the front loop of the cast-on stitch, wrap the yarn around the needle [figure 2] and pull a loop through, being careful not to interfere with the first garter ridge. Along the side of an incomplete square: When working along the side of an incomplete square, pick-knit one stitch under both loops of every selvedge stitch, beginning after the first/lowest garter ridge and ending in the outermost bind-off stitch.

[figure 1]

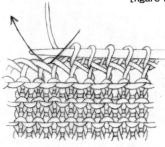

[figure 2]

TASSEL ▶

Cut a piece of cardboard 4" (10 cm) wide by the desired length of the tassel plus 1" (2.5 cm). Wrap yarn to desired thickness around cardboard. Cut a short length of yarn and tie it tightly around one end of the wrapped yarn **[figure 1]**. Cut the yarn loops at other end. Cut another piece of yarn and wrap it tightly around loops a short distance below the top knot to form the tassel neck. Knot the ends securely, then thread them onto a tapestry needle, and pull them to center of tassel **[figure 2]**. Trim the ends.

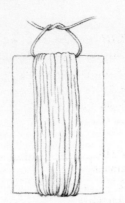

[figure 1]

[figure 2]

TURN WORK

Transfer the needle from your left hand to your right hand (as in picking up or knitting existing stitches after working a K-CO) or from your right hand to your left hand (as in working K-CO at the end of a row of knitting), then continue working as instructed.

WEAVE IN LOOSE ENDS ▼

With the end threaded on a tapestry needle, work along the diagonal, catching the back side of the stitches. To reduce bulk, do not weave two ends into the same area.

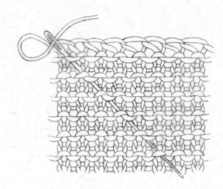

sources

YARN

Dale of Norway
N16 W23390 Stone Ridge Dr.,
Ste. A
Waukesha, WI 53188
www.dale.no

Baby Ull
Diamond Yarn
9697 St. Laurent, Ste. 101
Montreal, QC
Canada H3L 2N1
and
115 Martin Ross, Unit 3
Toronto, ON
Canada M3J 2L9
www.diamondyarn.com

Harrisville Designs
Center Village
PO Box 806
Harrisville, NH 03450
www.harrisville.com

Westminster Fibers/Rowan
165 Ledge St.
Nashua, NH 03060
www.westminsterfibers.com
In Canada: Diamond Yarn

Rauma Yarns
Available from:
Syvilla Tweed Bolson—
Tweeds & Fleece
512 Locust Rd.
Decorah, IA 52101
and
Arnhild's Knitting Studio
2315 Buchanan Dr.
Aimes, IA 50010
www.arnhild.com

Nordic Fiber Arts
4 Cutts Rd.
Durham, NH 03824
www.raumaull.no
Rauma Finullgarn

TOOLS FOR KNITTING AND FELTING

Clover Needlecraft Inc.
www.clover-usa.com

VIVIAN HØXBRO

www.viv.dk

index

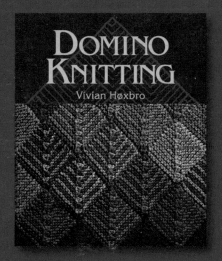